THE WORK OF JESUS CHRIST
AS AN ADVOCATE

THE WORK OF JESUS CHRIST AS AN ADVOCATE

CLEARLY EXPLAINED, AND LARGELY IMPROVED

FOR THE BENEFIT OF ALL BELIEVERS

And if any man sin, we have an advocate with the Father, Jesus Christ the righteous.—1 JOHN 2:1.

BY

JOHN BUNYAN

PUBLISHED BY

MINNEAPOLIS
2010

Published by Curiosmith.
P. O. Box 390293, Minneapolis, Minnesota, 55439.
Internet: curiosmith.com.
E-mail: shopkeeper@curiosmith.com.

Previously printed:
[London: Printed for Dorman Newman,
at the King's Arms, in the Poultry, 1688.]

All explanatory notes are from the George Offor Edition.
The in-text Bible references are footnoted in this edition.

Supplementary content and cover design:
Copyright © 2010 Charles J. Doe.

ISBN 9781935626091

CONTENTS

ADVERTISEMENT BY GEORGE OFFOR........................... 7
THE EPISTLE TO THE READER. 9
THE CONTENTS OF THIS TREATISE. 11
INTRODUCTION 19
1. WHEREIN CHRIST'S OFFICE AS ADVOCATE DOTH LIE........... 29
2. HOW CHRIST MANAGES THE OFFICE OF AN ADVOCATE........ 35
3. WHO HAVE CHRIST FOR AN ADVOCATE. 56
4. THE PRIVILEGES OF THOSE WHO HAVE CHRIST FOR AN ADVOCATE.. 73
5. THE NECESSITY OF HAVING CHRIST FOR OUR ADVOCATE. 90
6. OBJECTIONS REMOVED...................................... 105
7. THE USE AND APPLICATION................................. 112

ADVERTISEMENT BY GEORGE OFFOR

THIS is one of the most interesting of Bunyan's treatises, to edit which required the Bible at my right hand, and a law dictionary on my left. It was very frequently republished; but in an edition by John Marshall, 1725, it became most seriously mutilated, many passages were omitted, and numerous errors were made. In this state, it was copied into Mr. Whitefield's edition of his works, and it has been since republished with all those errors. It is now restored to its original state; and we hope that it will prove a most acceptable addition to our theological literature. Although Bunyan was shut up for more than twelve years a prisoner for the truth, and his time was so fully occupied in preaching, writing, and labouring to provide for the pressing wants of his family; still he managed to get acquainted, in a very remarkable manner, with all those law terms which are connected with the duties of a counsel, or advocate. He uses the words replevin, supersedeas, term, demur, nonsuit, reference, title, *in forma pauperis*, king's bench, common pleas, as properly and familiarly as if he had been brought up to the bar. How extraordinary must have been his mental powers, and how retentive his memory! I examined this work with apprehension, lest he had misapplied those hard words; but my surprise was great, to find that he had used every one of them with as much propriety as a Lord Chief-Justice could have done.

We are indebted for this treatise to Bunyan's having heard a sermon which excited his attention to a common, a dangerous, and a fatal heresy, more frequently preached to crowned heads, mitred prelates, members of parliament, and convocations, than it is to the poor, to whom *the gospel* is preached. In this sermon, the preacher said to his hearers, "see that your cause be good, else Christ will not undertake it." (Page 32.) Bunyan heard, as all Christians ought to hear, with careful jealousy, and at once detected the error. He exposes the fallacy, and uses his scriptural knowledge to confute it, by showing that Christ pleads for the wicked, the lost; for those who feel themselves so involved in a bad cause, that no advocate but Christ can bring them through. He manifests great anxiety that every inquirer should clearly ascertain definite truths and not be contented with general notions. (Pages 105–136.) This is very important advice, and by following which, we shall be saved from many painful doubts and fears. Our need of an advocate is proved by the fact, that Christ has undertaken the office. Some rely on their tears and sighs, as advocates for them with God; others on imperfect good works—from all these the soul must be shaken, until it finds that there is no prevailing Advocate but the Saviour; and that he alone, with his mystical body, the church, is entitled to the inheritance. Then sincere repentance, sighs, and tears, evidence our faith in him, and our godly sorrow for having occasioned him such inconceivable sufferings; tears of joy that we have such a Saviour and an Advocate, equally omnipotent to plead for, as to save us. The inheritance being Christ's, the members of his body cannot be cheated of it, or alienate it. (Page 100.) Bunyan, with his fertile imagination, and profound scriptural knowledge, spiritualizes the day of jubilee as a type of the safety of the inheritance of the saints. By our folly and sin we may lose sight for a time of our title deeds; but the inheritance is safe.

The whole work is a rich treat to those who love experimental divinity, and are safe in Christ as Noah was in the ark; but, Oh! how woeful must those be, who are without an interest in the Saviour; and that have none to plead their cause. "They are left to be ground to powder between the justice of God and the sins which they have committed. It is sad to consider their plight. This is the man that is pursued by the law, and by sin, and by death, and has none to plead his cause. Terrors take hold on him as waters; a stone hurleth him out of his place."[1] (Page 134.) Reader, this is a soul-searching subject—may it lead us to a solemn trial of our state, and to the happy conclusion, that the Saviour is our Advocate, and that our eternal inheritance is safe in heaven.

HACKNEY, *May* 1850.

GEORGE OFFOR

---

1 Job 27.

THE EPISTLE TO THE READER

Courteous Reader,

OF all the excellent offices which God the Father has conferred upon Jesus Christ our Lord, this of his being an Advocate with him for us is not the least, though, to the shame of saints it may be spoken, the blessed benefits thereof have not with that diligence and fervent desire been inquired after as they ought.

Christ, as sacrifice, priest, and king, with the glories in, and that flow from, him as such, has, God be thanked, in this our day, been much discovered by our seers, and as much rejoiced in by those who have believed their words; but as he is an Advocate with the Father, an Advocate for us, I fear the excellency of that doth still too much lie hid; though I am verily of opinion that the people of God in this age have as much need of the knowledge thereof, if not more need, than had their brethren that are gone before them.

These words, "if not more need," perhaps may seem to some to be somewhat out of joint; but let the godly wise consider the decays that are among us as to the power of godliness, and what abundance of foul miscarriages the generality of professors now stand guilty of, as also how diligent their great enemy is to accuse them at the bar of God for them, and I think they will conclude, that, in so saying, I indeed have said some truth. Wherefore, when I thought on this, and had somewhat considered also the transcendent excellency of the advocateship of this our Lord; and again, that but little of the glory thereof has by writing been, in our day, communicated to the church, I adventured to write what I have seen thereof, and do, by what doth follow, present it unto her for good.

I count not myself sufficient for this, or for any other truth as it is in Jesus; but yet, I say, I have told you somewhat of it, according to the proportion of faith. And I believe that some will thank God for what I here have said about it; but it will be chiefly those, whose right and title to the kingdom of heaven and glory, doth seem to themselves to be called in question by their enemy, at the bar of the Judge of all.

These, I say, will read, and be glad to hear, that they have an Advocate at court that will stand up to plead for them, and that will yet secure to them a right to the heavenly kingdom. Wherefore, it is more particularly for those that at present, or that hereafter, may be in this dreadful plight, that this my book is now made public; because it is, as I have showed, for such that Jesus Christ is Advocate with the Father.

Of the many and singular advantages, therefore, that such have by this their Advocate in his advocating for them, this book gives some account; as, where he pleads, how he pleads, what he pleads, when he pleads, with whom he pleads, for whom he pleads, and how the enemy is put to shame and silence before their God and all the holy angels.

Here is also showed to those herein concerned, how they indeed may know that Jesus is their Advocate; yea, and how their matters go before their God, the Judge; and particularly that they shall well come off at last, yea, though their cause, as it is theirs, is such, in justification of which, themselves do not dare to show their heads.

Nor have I left the dejected souls without directions how to entertain this Advocate to plead their cause; yea, I have also shown that he will be with ease prevailed with, to stand up to plead for such, as one would think, the very heavens would blush to hear them named by him. Their comfort also is, that he never lost a cause, nor a soul, for whom he undertook to be an Advocate with God.

But, reader, I will no longer detain thee from the perusal of the discourse. Read and think; read, and compare what thou readest with the Word of God. If thou findest any benefit by what thou readest, give the Father and his Son the glory; and also pray for me. If thou findest me short in this, or to exceed in that, impute all such things to my weakness, of which I am always full. Farewell. I am thine to serve thee what I may,

JOHN BUNYAN

THE CONTENTS OF THIS TREATISE
(PAGE NUMBERS ARE AFTER THE SECTIONS)

THE apostle's Divine policy, to beget a due regard to his Divine doctrine of eternal life.—The apostle's explication of this expression, viz., The blood of Jesus Christ cleanseth from all sin.—The apostle's exhortation to separation from sin, as a good effect of a good cause, viz., Forgiveness.—The apostle's addition, to prevent misunderstanding, viz., We have an advocate with the Father. (Page 19.)

    This brings to the text, in which are two great truths contained:
        I. A supposition, viz., That men in Christ may sin.
        II. An expression, by way of consolation, in case of sin, viz., We have an Advocate with the Father. (Page 20.)
    Two things for inquiry in these truths:
        First, An inquiry into what our apostle means by sin; in which is considered, A difference in the person and in the sin. And,
        Second, An inquiry into what it is for Christ to be an Advocate, viz., To plead for another in a court of judicature. (Page 21.)
    Seven things supposed in the office of an advocate:
        1. That God, as judge, is on the throne of judgment.
        2. That saints are concerned at that bar.
        3. That Christians have an accuser.
        4. That sinning saints dare not appear at this bar to plead their own cause.
        5. That Christians are apt to forget their Advocate, and remember their Judge.
        6. To remember our Advocate is the way to support faith and hope.

7. That if our advocate plead our cause (though that be never so black) he is able to bring us off. (Page 21.)

The apostle's triumph in Christ on this account.—An exhortation to the difficult task of believing.—Christ's advocateship declares us to be sorry creatures. (Page 26.)

THE METHOD OBSERVED IN THE DISCOURSE.

FIRST, TO SPEAK OF THIS ADVOCATE'S OFFICE. (Page 29.)

First, By touching on the nature of this office. (Page 29.)
Second, By treating of the order or place of this office. (Page 30.)
Third, The occasion of this office, viz., some great sin.—Christ, as Advocate, pleads a bad cause.—A good cause will plead for itself.—A bad man may have a good cause, and a good man may have a bad cause.—Christ, the righteous, pleading a bad cause, is a mystery.—The best saints are most sensible of their sins.—A pestilent passage of a preacher. (Page 31.)

SECOND, TO SHOW HOW CHRIST DOES MANAGE HIS OFFICE. (Page 35.)

First, How he manages his office of Advocate with the Father.
   1. ALONE, not by any proxy or deputy.
   2. Christ pleads at God's bar; the cause cannot be removed into another court.—If removed from heaven, we have no advocate on earth.
   3. In pleading, Christ observes these rules:
     (1.) He granteth what is charged on us.
     (2.) He pleads his own goodness for us.—He payeth all our debts down.—All mouths stopped, who would not have the sinner delivered.
     (3.) Christ requires a verdict in order to our deliverance.—The sinner is delivered, God contented, Satan confounded, and Christ applauded. (Page 35.)
Second, How Christ manages his office of an Advocate against the adversary by argument.
   1. He pleads the pleasure of his Father in his merits.—Satan rebuked for finding fault therewith.
   2. He pleads God's interest in his people.—Haman's mishap in being engaged against the king's queen.—N.B.

It seems a weak plea, because of man's unworthiness; but it is a strong plea, because of God's worthiness.—The elect are bound to God by a sevenfold cord.—The weight of the plea weighed. (Page 39.)

Third, Christ pleads his own interest in them.—A parallel between cattle in a pound and Christ's own sheep.—Six weighty reasons in this plea.
  1. They are Christ's own.
  2. They cost him dear.
  3. He hath made them near to himself.
   (*a*.) They are his spouse, his love, his dove; they are members of his body.
   (*b*.) A man cannot spare a hand, a foot, a finger. Nor can Christ spare any member.
  4. Christ pleads his right in heaven to give it to whom he will.—Christ will; Satan will not; Christ's will stands.
  5. Christ pleads Satan's enmity against the godly.—Satan is the cause of the crimes he accuses us of.—A simile of a weak-witted child.
  6. Christ can plead those sins of saints for them for which Satan would have them damned.—Eight considerations to clear that.—Seven more considerations to the same end.—Men care most for children that are infirm.—A father offended hath been appeased by a brother turning advocate. (Page 44.)

THIRD HEAD.—TO SHOW WHO HAVE CHRIST FOR AN ADVOCATE; WHEREIN ARE THREE THINGS CONTAINED. (Page 56.)

First, This office of advocate differs from that of a priest.
  1. They differ in name.
  2. They differ in nature.
  3. They differ as to their extent.
  4. They differ as to the persons with whom they have to do.
  5. They differ as to the matter about which they are employed.
  6. Christ, as Priest, precedes; Christ, as Advocate, succeeds. (Page 56.)
Second, How far this office of an advocate is extended; in five particulars. (Page 57.)

Third, Who have Christ for their Advocate.
1. In general, all adopted children.—*Objection.* The text saith, "If any man sin."—*Answer.* "Any man," is not any of the world; but any of the children of God.—A difference in children; some bigger than some.—Christ an Advocate for strong men.
2. In particular, to show if Christ be our Advocate.
    (1.) If one have entertained Christ to plead a cause.—*Question.* How shall I know that?—*Answer.* By being sensible of an action commenced against thee in the high court of justice.
    (2.) If one have revealed a cause to Christ.—An example of one revealing his cause to Christ, in a closet.—In order to this, one must know Christ.
    (*a.*) To be a friend.
    (*b.*) To be faithful.
    (3.) If one have committed a cause to Christ.—In order to this, one must be convinced.
    (a.) Of Christ's ability to defend him.
    (*b.*) Of Christ's courage to plead a cause.
    (*c.*) Of Christ's will for this work.
    (*d.*) Of Christ's tenderness in case of his client's dulness.
    (*e.*) Of Christ's unweariedness.
    (4.) If one wait till things come to a legal issue.—*Question.* What is it thus to wait?—*Answer.*
    (*a.*) To be of good courage; look for deliverance.
    (*b.*) To keep his way in waiting.
    (*c.*) To observe his directions.
    (*d.*) To hearken to further directions which may come from the advocate.
    (*e.*) To come to no ill conclusion in waiting, viz., that the cause is lost; because one hears not from court.
    (*f.*) To wait waking, not sleeping.—Ordinances and ministers compared to a post house and carriers of letters.—The client's comfortable conclusion about his advocate and cause.—But yet doubting and desponding.—The author's reply to, and compliance with, the client's conclusion; and his counsel in the case. (Page 58.)

FOURTH HEAD.—TO SHOW THE CLIENT'S PRIVILEGES, BY THE BENEFIT OF THIS OFFICE OF ADVOCATE. (Page 73.)

First Privilege.—The Advocate pleads a price paid.—Of a rich brother and his poor brethren.—Of the ill-conditioned man, their enemy.—Further cleared by three considerations. (Page 73.)

Second Privilege.—The client's Advocate pleads for himself also; both concerned in one bottom.
1. He pleads the price of his own blood.
2. He pleads it for his own.—A simile of a lame horse.—Of men going to law for a thing of little worth.—*Objection.* I am but one.—*Answer.* Christ cannot lose one. (Page 75.)

Third Privilege.—The plea of Satan is groundless.—Satan must be cast over the bar.—A simile of a widow owing a sum of money.—Of an old law nulled[1] by a new law.—Satan pleads by the old law; Christ by the new. (Page 77.)

Fourth Privilege.—Is consequential; the client's accuser must needs be overthrown.—The client's solemn appeal to the Almighty.—In case the accused have no advocate, Satan prevails. (Page 80.)

Fifth Privilege.—The Advocate hath pity for his client, and indignation against the accuser.—Men choose an advocate who hath a quarrel against their adversary. (Page 81.)

Sixth Privilege.—The judge counts the accuser his enemy.—To procure the judge's son to plead, is desirable. (Page 82.)

Seventh Privilege.—The client's Advocate hath good courage; he will set his face like a flint.—He pleads before the God, and all the host, of heaven.—He is the old friend of publicans and sinners.—He pleads a cause bad enough to make angels blush.—Love will do, and bear, and suffer much. (Page 82.)

Eighth Privilege.—The Advocate is always ready in court.—He appears NOW in the presence of God. (Page 84.)

Ninth Privilege.—The Advocate will not be blinded with bribes. (Page 86.)

Tenth Privilege.—The Advocate is judge in the client's cause.—Joseph's exaltation was Israel's advantage.—God's care of his people's welfare. (Page 87.)

---

1 Nulled—repealed or annulled.—(OFFOR.)

Eleventh Privilege.—The Advocate hath all that is requisite for an advocate to have. (Page 88.)

FIFTH.—LAST HEAD.—TO SHOW THE NECESSITY OF CHRIST FOR OUR ADVOCATE. (Page 90.)

First.—To vindicate the justice of God against the cavils of the devil.—Satan charges God with unjust words and actions.—God is pleased with his design to save sinners. (Page 90.)

Second.—There is law to be objected against us.—Christ appeals to the law itself.—Christ is not ashamed to own the way of salvation. (Page 92.)

Third.—Many things give our accuser advantage.
  1. Many things relating to the promises.
  2. Many things relating to our lives.
  3. The threats annexed to the gospel. (Page 94.)

Fourth.—To plead about our afflictions for sins.—A simile of a man indicted at the assizes, and his malicious adversary.—An allusion to Abishai and Shimei, who cursed David. (Page 98.)

Fifth.—To plead the efficacy of our old titles to our inheritance, if questionable because of new sins.—Saints do not sell their inheritance by sin. (Page 100.)

Sixth.—Our evidences are oft out of our hand, and we recover them by our Advocate. (Page 102.)

SIXTH.—OBJECTIONS REMOVED. (Page 105.)

First Objection.—What need all these offices or nice distinctions.—*Answer.* The wisdom of God is not to be charged with folly.—God's people are baffled with the devil for want of a distinct knowledge of Christ in all his offices. (Page 105.)

Second Objection.—My cause being bad, Christ will desert me.—*Answer.* Sin is deadly destruction to faith.—A fivefold order observed in the exercise of faith. (Page 106.)

Third Objection.—But who shall pay the Advocate his fee?—*Answer.* There is law, and lawyers too, without money.—Christ pleads for the poor.—David's strange gift to God. (Page 108.)

Fourth Objection.—If Christ be my Advocate once, he will always be troubled with me.—*Answer.* He is an Advocate to the utmost. (Page 110.)

SEVENTH.—USE AND APPLICATION. (Page 112.)

Use First.—To consider the dignity God hath put upon Christ, by offices, places of trust, and titles of honour, in general. (Page 112.)

Use Second.—To consider this office of an Advocate in particular; by which consideration these advantages come:
1. To see one is not forsaken for sin.
2. To take courage to contend with the devil.
3. It affords relief for discouraged faith.
4. It helps to put off the vizor Satan puts on Christ.—A simile of a vizor on the face of a father.—Study this peculiar treasure of an advocate.
    (1.) With reference to its peculiarity.
    (2.) Study the nature of this office.
    (3.) Study its efficacy and prevalency.
    (4.) Study Christ's faithfulness in his office.
    (5.) Study the need of a share therein. (Page 115.)

Use Third.—To wonder at Christ's condescension, in being an Advocate for the base and unworthy.—Christ acts in open court,
1. With a holy and just God.
2. Before all the heavenly host.
3. The client is unconcerned for whom the Advocate is engaged.
4. The majesty of the man that is an Advocate. (Page 120.)

Use Fourth.—Improve this doctrine to strengthen grace.
1. To strengthen faith.
2. To encourage to prayer.
3. To keep humble.
4. To encourage to perseverance.—*Objection.* I cannot pray; my mouth is stopped.—*Answer.* Satan cannot silence Christ.
5. Improve this doctrine, to drive difficulties down. (Page 123.)

Use Fifth.—If Christ pleads for us before God, we should plead for him before men.—Nine considerations to that end.—The last reserve for a dead lift. (Page 127.)

Use Sixth.—To be wary of sin against God.—Christianity teaches ingenuity.[1]—Christ is our Advocate, on free cost.—A comely conclusion of a brute.—Three considerations added. (Page 129.)

Use Seventh.—The strong are to tell the weak of an Advocate to plead their cause.—A word in season is good. (Page 132.)

Use Eighth.—All is nothing to them that have none to plead their cause.—An instance of God's terrible judgment.—*Objection.* There is grace, the promise, the blood of Christ; cannot these save, except Christ be Advocate?—*Answer.* These, and Advocate, and all, little enough.—Christ no Advocate for such as have no sense of, and shame for sin.—*Objection.* Is not Christ an Advocate for his elect uncalled?—*Answer.* He died, and prayeth, for all his elect, as Priest; as Advocate, pleads for the called only. (Page 133.)

---

1 Ingenuity—ingenuousness, frankness, *sincerity*.—(Offor.)

THE WORK OF JESUS CHRIST AS AN ADVOCATE

And if any man sin, we have an advocate with the father, Jesus Christ the righteous.—1 JOHN 2:1.

THAT the apostle might obtain due regard from those to whom he wrote, touching the things about which he wrote, he tells them that he received not his message to them at second or third hand, but was himself an eye and ear witness thereof—"That which was from the beginning, which we have heard, which we have seen with our eyes, which we have looked upon, and our hands have handled, of the word of life, (for the life was manifested, and we have seen *it*, and bear witness and show unto you that eternal life, which was with the Father, and was manifested unto us;) that which we have seen and heard, declare we unto you."[1] Having thus told them of his ground for what he said, he proceeds to tell them also the matter contained in his errand—to wit, that he brought them news of eternal life, as freely offered in the word of the gospel to them; or rather, that that gospel which they had received would certainly usher them in at the gates of the kingdom of heaven, were their reception of it sincere and in truth—for, saith he, then "the blood of Jesus Christ the Son of God cleanseth you from all sin."

Having thus far told them what was his errand, he sets upon an explication of what he had said, especially touching

---

1 How deeply important is this essential doctrine of Christianity—a personal investigation. We must hear and see for ourselves, handle the word of life, and not trust to others, however holy and capable they may appear to be; we must search the Scriptures, and pray for ourselves, or we have not the slightest claim to the name of Christian.—(OFFOR.)

our being cleansed from all sin—"Not," saith he, "from a being of sin; for should we say so, we should deceive ourselves," and should prove that we have no truth of God in us, but by cleansing, I mean a being delivered from all sin, so as that none at all shall have the dominion over you, to bring you down to hell; for that, for the sake of the blood of Christ, all trespasses are forgiven you.

This done, he exhorts them to shun or fly sin, and not to consent to the motions, workings, enticings, or allurements thereof, saying, "I write unto you that ye sin not." Let not forgiveness have so bad an effect upon you as to cause you to be remiss in Christian duties, or as to tempt you to give way to evil. Shall we sin because we are forgiven? or shall we not much matter what manner of lives we live, because we are set free from the law of sin and death? God forbid. Let grace teach us another lesson, and lay other obligations upon our spirits. "My little children," saith he, "these things write I unto you, that ye sin not." What things? Why, tidings of pardon and salvation, and of that nearness to God, to which you are brought by the precious blood of Christ. Now, lest also by this last exhortation he should yet be misunderstood, he adds, "And if any man sin, we have an Advocate with the Father, Jesus Christ the righteous." I say, he addeth this to prevent desponding in those weak and sensible Christians that are so quick of feeling and of discerning the corruptions of their natures; for these cry out continually that there is nothing that they do but it is attended with sinful weaknesses.

Wherefore, in the words we are presented with two great truths—I. With a supposition, that men in Christ, while in this world, may sin—"If any man sin;" any man; none are excluded; for all, or any one of the all of them that Christ hath redeemed and forgiven, are incident to sin. By "may" I mean, not a toleration, but a possibility; "For *there* is not a man, not a just man upon earth, that doeth good, and sinneth not."[1] II. The other thing with which we are presented is, an Advocate—"If any man sin, we have an Advocate with the Father, Jesus Christ the righteous."

Now there lieth in these two truths two things to be inquired into, as—*First*, What the apostle should here mean by sin. *Second*, And also, what he here doth mean by an advocate—"If

---
1 Ecclesiastes 7:20; 1 Kings 8:46.

any man sin, we have an Advocate." There is ground to inquire after the first of these, because, though here he saith, they that sin have an advocate, yet in the very next chapter he saith, "Such are of the devil, have not seen God, neither know him, nor are of him." There is ground also to inquire after the second, because an advocate is supposed in the text to be of use to them that sin—"If any man sin, we have an Advocate."

First, For the first of these—to wit, what the apostle should here mean by sin—"If any man sin."

I answer, since there is a difference in the persons, there must be a difference in the sin. That there is a difference in the persons is showed before; one is called a child of God, the other is said to be of the wicked one. Their sins differ also, in their degree at least; for no child of God sins to that degree as to make himself incapable of forgiveness; for "he that is begotten of God keepeth himself, and that wicked one toucheth him not."[1] Hence, the apostle says, "There is a sin unto death."[2] Which is the sin from which he that is born of God is kept. The sins therefore are thus distinguished: The sins of the people of God are said to be sins that men commit, the others are counted those which are the sins of devils.

1. The sins of God's people are said to be sins which men commit, and for which they have an Advocate, though they who sin after the example of the wicked one have none. "When a man or woman," saith Moses, "shall commit any sin that men commit . . . they shall confess their sin . . . and an atonement shall be made for him."[3] Mark, it is when they commit a sin which men commit; or, as Hosea has it, When they transgress the commandment like Adam.[4] Now, these are the sins under consideration by the apostle, and to deliver us from which, "we have an Advocate with the Father."

2. But for the sins mentioned in the third chapter, since the persons sinning go here under another character, they also must be of another stamp—to wit, a making head against the person, merits, and grace of Jesus Christ. These are the sins of devils in the world, and for these there is no remission. These, they also that are of the wicked one commit, and therefore sin

---

[1] 1 John 5:18.
[2] 1 John 5:16. See also Matthew 12:32.
[3] Numbers 5:5–7.
[4] Hosea 6:7.

after the similitude of Satan, and so fall into the condemnation of the devil.

Second, But what is it for Jesus to be an Advocate for these? "If any man sin, we have an Advocate."

An advocate is one who pleadeth for another at any bar, or before any court of judicature; but of this more in its place. So, then, we have in the text a Christian, as supposed, committing sin, and a declaration of an Advocate prepared to plead for him—"If any man sin, we have an Advocate with the Father."

And this leads me first to inquire into what, by these words the apostle must, of necessity, presuppose? For making use here of the similitude or office of an advocate, thereby to show the preservation of the sinning Christian, he must,

1. Suppose that God, as judge, is now upon the throne of his judgment; for an advocate is to plead at a bar, before a court of judicature. Thus it is among men; and forasmuch as our Lord Jesus is said to be an "Advocate with the Father," it is clear that there is a throne of judgment also. This the prophet Micaiah affirms, saying, "I saw the Lord sitting on his throne, and all the host of heaven standing by him on his right hand and on his left."[1] Sitting upon a throne for judgment; for from the Lord, as then sitting upon that throne, proceeded that sentence against king Ahab, that he should go and fall at Ramoth-gilead; and he did go, and did fall there, as the award or fruit of that judgment. That is the first.

2. The text also supposeth that the saints as well as sinners are concerned at that bar; for the apostle saith plainly that there "we have an Advocate." And the saints are concerned at that bar; because they transgress as well as others, and because the law is against the sin of saints as well as against the sins of other men. If the saints were not capable of committing of sin, what need would they have of an advocate?[2,3] Yea, though they did sin, yet if they were by Christ so set free from the law as that it could by no means take cognizance of their sins, what need would they have of an advocate? None at all. If there be twenty places where there are assizes kept in this land, yet if I have offended no law, what need have I of an advocate?

---

1 1 Kings 22:19.

2 1 Chronicles 21:3–6; 1 Samuel 12:13–14.

3 The sin here referred to was numbering the people of Israel; see 1 Chronicles 21:1.—(Offor.)

especially if the judge be just, and knows me altogether, as the God of heaven does? But here is a Judge that is just; and here is an Advocate also, an Advocate for the children, an Advocate to plead; for an advocate as such is not of use but before a bar to plead; therefore, here is an offence, and so a law broken by the saints as well as others. That is the second thing.

3. As the text supposes that there is a judge, and crimes of saints, so it supposeth that there is an accuser, one that will carefully gather up the faults of good men, and that will plead them at this bar against them. Hence we read of "the accuser of our brethren, that accused them before our God day and night."[1] For Satan doth not only tempt the godly man to sin, but, having prevailed with him, and made him guilty, he packs away to the court, to God the judge of all; and there addresses himself to accuse that man, and to lay to his charge the heinousness of his offence, pleading against him the law that he has broken, the light against which he did it, and the like. But now, for the relief and support of such poor people, the apostle, by the text, presents them with an advocate; that is, with one to plead for them, while Satan pleads against them; with one that pleads for pardon, while Satan, by accusing, seeks to pull judgment and vengeance upon our heads. "If any man sin, we have an Advocate with the Father, Jesus Christ the righteous." That is the third thing.

4. As the apostle supposeth a judge, crimes, and an accuser, so he also supposeth that those herein concerned—to wit, the sinning children—neither can nor dare attempt to appear at this bar themselves to plead their own cause before this Judge and against this accuser; for if they could or durst do this, what need they have an advocate? for an advocate is of use to them whose cause themselves neither can nor dare appear to plead. Thus Job prayed for an advocate to plead his cause with God,[2] and David cries out, "Enter not into judgment with thy servant," O God, "for in thy sight shall no man living be justified."[3] Wherefore, it is evident that saints neither can nor dare adventure to plead their cause. Alas! the Judge is the almighty and eternal God; the law broken is the holy and perfect rule of God, in itself a consuming fire. The sin is so odious, and a thing so

---

1 Revelation 12:10–12.
2 Job 16:21.
3 Psalm 143:2.

abominable, that it is enough to make all the angels blush to hear it but so much as once mentioned in so holy a place as that is where this great God doth sit to judge. This sin now hangs about the neck of him that hath committed it; yea, it covereth him as doth a mantle. The adversary is bold, cunning, and audacious, and can word a thousand of us into an utter silence in less than half a quarter of an hour. What, then, should the sinner, if he could come there, do at this bar to plead? Nothing; nothing for his own advantage. But now comes in his mercy—he has an Advocate to plead his cause—"If any man sin, we have an Advocate with the Father, Jesus Christ the righteous." That is the fourth thing. But again,

5. The apostle also supposeth by the text there is an aptness in Christians when they have sinned, to forget that they "have an Advocate with the Father;" wherefore this is written to put them in remembrance—"If any man sin, (let him remember) we have an Advocate." We can think of all other things well enough—namely, that God is a just judge, that the law is perfectly holy, that my sin is a horrible and an abominable thing, and that I am certainly thereof accused before God by Satan.

These things, I say, we readily think of, and forget them not. Our conscience puts us in mind of these, our guilt puts us in mind of these, the devil puts us in mind of these, and our reason and sense hold the knowledge and remembrance of these close to us. All that we forget is, that we have an Advocate, "an Advocate with the Father"—that is, one that is appointed to take in hand in open court, before all the angels of heaven, my cause, and to plead it by such law and arguments as will certainly fetch me off, though I am clothed with filthy garments; but this, I say, we are apt to forget, as Job when he said, "O that one might plead for a man with God, as a man *pleadeth* for his neighbour!"[1] Such an one Job had, but he had almost at this time forgot it; as he seems to intimate also where he wisheth for a daysman that might lay his hand upon them both.[2] But our mercy is, we have one to plead our cause, "an Advocate with the Father, Jesus Christ the righteous," who will not suffer our soul to be spilt and spoiled before the throne, but will surely plead our cause.

6. Another thing that the apostle would have us learn from

---

1 Job 16:21.
2 Job 9:33.

the words is this, that to remember and to believe that Jesus Christ is an Advocate for us when we have sinned, is the next way to support and strengthen our faith and hope. Faith and hope are very apt to faint when our sins in their guilt do return upon us; nor is there any more proper way to relieve our souls than to understand that the Son of God is our Advocate in heaven. True, Christ died for our sins as a sacrifice, and as a priest he sprinkleth with his blood the mercy-seat; ay, but here is one that has sinned after profession of faith, that has sinned grievously, so grievously that his sins are come up before God; yea, are at his bar pleaded against him by the accuser of the brethren, by the enemy of the godly. What shall he do now? Why, let him believe in Christ. Believe, that is true; but how now must he conceive in his mind of Christ for the encouraging of him so to do? Why, let him call to mind that Jesus Christ is an Advocate with the Father, and as such he meeteth the accuser at the bar of God, pleads for this man that has sinned against this accuser, and prevaileth for ever against him. Here now, though Satan be turned lawyer, though he accuseth, yea, though his charge against us is true, (for suppose that we have sinned,) "yet our Advocate is with the Father, Jesus Christ the righteous." Thus is faith encouraged, thus is hope strengthened, thus is the spirit of the sinking Christian revived, and made to wait for a good deliverance from a bad cause and a cunning adversary; especially if you consider,

7. That the apostle doth also further suppose by the text that Jesus Christ, as Advocate, if he will but plead our cause, let that be never so black, is able to bring us off, even before God's judgment-seat, to our joy, and the confounding of our adversary; for when he saith, "We have an Advocate," he speaks nothing if he means not thus. But he doth mean thus, he must mean thus, because he seeketh here to comfort and support the fallen. "Has any man sinned? We have an Advocate." But what of that, if yet he be unable to fetch us off when charged for sin at the bar, and before the face of a righteous judge?

But he is able to do this. The apostle says so, in that he supposes a man has sinned, as any man among the godly ever did; for so we may understand it; and if he giveth us not leave to understand it so, he saith nothing to the purpose neither, for it will be objected, by some—But can he fetch me off, though I have done as David, as Solomon, as Peter, or the like? It must be answered, Yes. The openness of the terms ANY MAN, the indefiniteness of the word SIN, doth naturally allow us to take him in the largest sense; besides, he brings in this saying as the chief, most apt, and fittest to relieve one crushed down to death and hell by the guilt of sin and a wounded conscience.

Further, methinks by these words the apostle seems to triumph in his Christ, saying, My brethren, I would have you study to be holy; but if your adversary the devil should get the advantage of you, and besmear you with the filth of sin, you have yet, besides all that you have heard already, "an Advocate with the Father, Jesus Christ the righteous," who is as to his person, in interest with God, his wisdom and worth, able to bring you off, to the comforting of your souls.

Let me, therefore, for a conclusion as to this, give you an exhortation to believe, to hope, and expect, that though you have sinned, (for now I speak to the fallen saint) that Jesus Christ will make a good end with thee—"Trust," I say, "in him, and he shall bring it to pass." I know I put thee upon a hard and difficult task for believing and expecting good, when my guilty conscience doth nothing but clog, burden, and terrify me with the justice of God, the greatness of thy sins, and the burning torments is hard and sweating work. But it must be; the text calls for it, thy case calls for it, and thou must do it, if thou wouldst glorify Christ; and this is the way to hasten the issue of thy cause in hand, for believing daunts the devil, pleaseth Christ, and will help thee beforehand to sing that song of the church, saying, "O Lord, thou hast pleaded the causes of my soul; thou hast redeemed my life."[1] Yea, believe, and hear thy pleading Lord say to thee, "Thus saith thy Lord the Lord, and thy God *that* pleadeth the cause of his people, Behold, I have taken out of thine hand the cup of trembling, *even* the dregs of the cup of my fury; thou shalt no more drink it again."[2] I am not here discoursing of the sweetness of Christ's nature, but of the excellency of his offices, and of his office of advocateship in particular, which, as a lawyer for his client, he is to execute in the presence of God for us. Love may be where there is no office, and so where no power is to do us good; but now, when love and office shall meet, they will surely both combine in Christ to do the fallen Christian good. But of his love we have treated elsewhere; we will here discourse of the office of

---

1 Lamentations 3:58.
2 Isaiah 51:22.

this loving one. And for thy further information, let me tell thee that God thy Father counteth that thou wilt be, when compared with his law, but a poor one all thy days; yea, the apostle tells thee so, in that he saith there is an Advocate provided for thee. When a father provides crutches for his child, he doth as good as say, I count that my child will be yet infirm; and when God shall provide an Advocate, he doth as good as say, My people are subject to infirmities. Do not, therefore, think of thyself above what, by plain texts, and fair inferences drawn from Christ's offices, thou are bound to think. What doth it bespeak concerning thee that Christ is always a priest in heaven, and there ever lives to make intercession for thee,[1] but this, that thou art at the best in thyself, yea, and in thy best exercising of all thy graces too, but a poor, pitiful, sorry, sinful man; a man that would, when yet most holy, be certainly cast away, did not thy high priest take away for thee the iniquity of thy holy things. The age we live in is a wanton age; the godly are not so humble, and low, and base in their own eyes as they should, though their daily experience calls for it, and the priesthood of Jesus Christ too.

But above all, the advocateship of Jesus Christ declares us to be sorry creatures; for that office does, as it were, predict that some time or other we shall basely fall, and by falling be undone, if the Lord Jesus stand not up to plead. And as it shows this concerning us, so it shows concerning God that he will not lightly or easily lose his people. He has provided well for us—blood to wash us in; a priest to pray for us, that we may be made to persevere; and, in case we foully fall, an advocate to plead our cause, and to recover us from under, and out of all that danger, that by sin and Satan, we at any time may be brought into.

But having thus briefly passed through that in the text which I think the apostle must necessarily presuppose, I shall now endeavour to enter into the bowels of it, and see what, in a more particular manner, shall be found therein. And, for my more profitable doing of this work, I shall choose to observe this method in my discourse—

METHOD OF THE DISCOURSE.

FIRST, I shall show you more particularly of this Advocate's office, or what and wherein Christ's office as Advocate doth lie.

---
1 Hebrews 7:24.

SECOND, After that, I shall also show you how Jesus Christ doth manage this office of an Advocate. THIRD, I shall also then show you who they are that have Jesus Christ for their Advocate. FOURTH, I shall also show you what excellent privileges they have, who have Jesus Christ for their Advocate. FIFTH, And to silence cavillers, I shall also show the necessity of this office of Jesus Christ. SIXTH, I shall come to answer some objections; and, LASTLY, To the use and application.

WHEREIN CHRIST'S OFFICE AS ADVOCATE DOTH LIE

FIRST, To begin with the first of these—namely, *to show you more particularly of Christ's office as an Advocate, and wherein it lieth*; the which I shall do these three ways—*First*, Touch again upon the nature of this office; and then, *Second*, Treat of the order and place that it hath among the rest of his offices; and, *Third*, Treat of the occasion of the execution of this office.

First, To touch upon the nature of this office. It is that which empowereth a man to plead for a man, or one man to plead for another; not in common discourses, and upon common occasions, as any man may do, but at a bar, or before a court of judicature, where a man is accused or impleaded by his enemy; I say, this Advocate's office is such, both here, and in the kingdom of heaven. An advocate is as one of our attorneys, at least in the general, who pleads according to law and justice for one or other that is in trouble by reason of some miscarriage, or of the naughty temper of some that are about him, who trouble and vex, and labour to bring him into danger of the law. This is the nature of this office, as I said, on earth; and this is the office that Christ executeth in heaven. Wherefore he saith, "If any man sin, we have an Advocate;" one to stand up for him, and to plead for his deliverance before the bar of God.[1]

For though in some places of Scripture Christ is said to plead for his with men, and that by terrible arguments, as by fire, and sword, and famine, and pestilence, yet this is not that which is intended by this text; for the apostle here saith, he is an Advocate with the Father, or before the Father, to plead for those that there, or that to the Father's face, shall be accused for their transgressions: "If any man sin, we have an Advocate

---

1 Joel 3:2; Isaiah 66:16; Ezekiel 38:22; Jeremiah 2.

with the Father, Jesus Christ the righteous." So, then, this is the employ of Jesus Christ as he is for us, an Advocate. He has undertaken to stand up for his people at God's bar, and before that great court, there to plead, by the law and justice of heaven, for their deliverance; when, for their faults, they are accused, indicted, or impleaded by their adversary.

Second. And now to treat of the order or place that this office of Christ hath among the rest of his offices, which he doth execute for us while we are here in a state of imperfection; and I think it is an office that is to come behind as a reserve, or for a help at last, when all other means shall seem to fail. Men do not use to go to law upon every occasion; or if they do, the wisdom of the judge, the jury, and the court will not admit that every brangle and foolish quarrel shall come before them; but an Advocate doth then come into place, and then to the exercise of his office, when a cause is counted worthy to be taken notice of by the judge and by the court. Wherefore he, I say, comes in the last place, as a reserve, or help at last, to plead; and, by pleading, to set that right by law which would otherwise have caused an increase to more doubts, and to further dangers.

Christ, as priest, doth always works of service for us, because in our most spiritual things there may faults and spots be found, and these he taketh away of course, by the exercise of that office; for he always wears that plate of gold upon his forehead before the Father, whereon is written, "Holiness to the Lord." But now, besides these common infirmities, there are faults that are highly gross and foul, that oft are found in the skirts of the children of God. Now, these are they that Satan taketh hold on; these are they that Satan draweth up a charge against us for; and to save us from these, it is, that the Lord Jesus is made an Advocate. When Joshua was clothed with filthy garments, then Satan stood at his right hand to resist him; then the angel of the covenant, the Lord Jesus, pleaded for his help.[1] By all which it appears, that this office comes behind, is provided as a reserve, that we may have help at a pinch, and then be lifted out, when we sink in mire, where there is no standing.

This is yet further hinted at by the several postures that Christ is said to be in, as he exerciseth his priestly and advocate's office. As a Priest, he sits; as an Advocate, he stands.[2] The Lord

---

1 Zechariah 3.
2 Isaiah 3:13.

stands up when he pleads; his sitting is more constant and of course (Sit thou,[1]), but his standing is occasional, when Joshua is indicted, or when hell and earth are broken loose against his servant Stephen. For as Joshua was accused by the devil, and as then the angel of the Lord stood by, so when Stephen was accused by men on earth, and that charge seconded by the fallen angels before the face of God, it is said, "the Lord Jesus stood on the right hand of God,"[2]—to wit, to plead; for so I take it, because standing is his posture as an Advocate, not as a Priest; for, as a Priest, he must sit down; but he standeth as an Advocate, as has been showed afore.[3] Wherefore,

Third. The occasion of his exercising of this office of advocate is, as hath been hinted already, when a child of God shall be found guilty before God of some heinous sin, of some grievous thing in his life and conversation. For as for those infirmities that attend the best, in their most spiritual sacrifices; if a child of God were guilty of ten thousand of them, they are of course purged, through the much incense that is always mixed with those sacrifices in the golden censer that is in the hand of Christ; and so he is kept clean, and counted upright, notwithstanding those infirmities; and, therefore, you shall find that, notwithstanding those common faults, the children of God are counted good and upright in conversation, and not charged as offenders. "David" saith the text, "did *that which was* right in the eyes of the Lord, and turned not aside from any *thing* that he commanded him, all the days of his life, save only in the matter of Uriah the Hitite."[4] But was David, in a strict sense, without fault in all things else? No, verily; but that was foul in a higher degree than the rest, and therefore there God sets a blot; ay, and doubtless for that he was accused by Satan before the throne of God; for here is adultery, and murder, and hypocrisy, in David's doings; here is notorious matter, a great sin, and so a great ground for Satan to draw up an indictment against the king; and a thundering one, to be sure, shall be preferred against him. This is the time, then, for Christ to stand up to plead; for now there is room for such a question—Can David's sin stand with grace? or, Is it possible that a man that has done as he has, should yet be found

---

1 Psalm 110:1, 4.
2 Acts 7:55.
3 Hebrews 10:12.
4 1 Kings 15:5.

a saint, and so in a saved state? or, Can God repute him so, and yet be holy and just? or, Can the merits of the Lord Jesus reach, according to the law of heaven, a man in this condition? Here is a case dubious; here is a man whose salvation, by his foul offences, is made doubtful; now we must to law and judgment, wherefore now let Christ stand up to plead! I say, now was David's case dubious; he was afraid that God would cast him away, and the devil hoped he would, and to that end charged him before God's face, if, perhaps, he might get sentence of damnation to pass upon his soul.[1] But this was David's mercy, he had an Advocate to plead his cause, by whose wisdom and skill in matters of law and judgment he was brought off of those heavy charges, from those gross sins, and delivered from that eternal condemnation, that by the law of sin and death, was due thereto.

This is then the occasion that Christ taketh to plead, as Advocate, for the salvation of his people—to wit, the cause: He "pleadeth the cause of his people."[2] Not every cause, but such and such a cause; the cause that is very bad, and by the which they are involved, not only in guilt and shame, but also in danger of death and hell. I say, the cause is bad, if the text be true, if sin can make it bad, yea, if sin itself be bad—"If any man sin, we have an Advocate;" an Advocate to plead for him; for him as considered guilty, and so, consequently, as considered in a bad condition. It is true, we must distinguish between the person and the sin; and Christ pleads for the person, not the sin; but yet He cannot be concerned with the person, but he must be with the sin; for though the person and the sin may be distinguished, yet they cannot be separated. He must plead, then, not for a person only, but for a guilty person, for a person under the worst of circumstances—"If any man sin, we have an Advocate" for him as so considered.

When a man's cause is good, it will sufficiently plead for itself, yea, and for its master too, especially when it is made appear so to be, before a just and righteous judge. Here, therefore, needs no advocate; the judge himself will pronounce him righteous. This is evidently seen in Job—"Thou movedst me against him (this said God to Satan), to destroy him without cause."[3] Thus far Job's cause was good, wherefore he did not

---

1 Psalm 51.
2 Isaiah 51:22.
3 Job 2:3.

need an advocate; his cause pleaded for itself, and for its owner also. But if it was to plead good causes for which Christ is appointed Advocate, then the apostle should have written thus: If any man be righteous, we have an Advocate with the Father. Indeed, I never heard but one in all my life preach from this text, and he, when he came to handle the cause for which he was to plead, pretended it must be good, and therefore said to the people, See that your cause be good, else Christ will not undertake it. But when I heard it, Lord, thought I, if this be true, what shall I do, and what will become of all this people, yea, and of this preacher too? Besides, I saw by the text, the apostle supposeth another cause, a cause bad, exceeding bad, if sin can make it so. And this was one cause why I undertook this work.

When we speak of a cause, we speak not of a person simply as so considered; for, as I said before, person and cause must be distinguished; nor can the person make the cause good but as he regulates his action by the Word of God. If, then, a good, a righteous, man doth what the law condemns, that thing is bad; and if he be indicted for so doing, he is indicted for a bad cause; and he that will be his advocate, must be concerned in and about a bad matter; and how he will bring his client off, therein doth lie the mystery.

I know that a bad man may have a good cause depending before the judge, and so also good men have.[1] But then they are bold in their own cause, and fear not to make mention of it, and in Christ to plead their innocency before the God of heaven, as well as before men.[2] But we have in the text a cause that all men are afraid of—a cause that the apostle concludes so bad that none but Jesus Christ himself can save a Christian from it. It is not only sinful, but sin itself—"If any man sin, we have an Advocate with the Father."

Wherefore there is in this place handled by the apostle, one of the greatest mysteries under heaven—to wit, that an innocent and holy Jesus should take in hand to plead for one before a just and righteous God, that has defiled himself with sin; yea, that he should take in hand to plead for such an one against the fallen angels, and that he should also by his plea effectually rescue, and bring them off from the crimes and curse whereof they were verily guilty by the verdict of the law, and approbation of the Judge.

---

1 Job 31.
2 Psalm 71:3–5; 2 Corinthians 1:23; Galatians 1:10; Philippians 1:8.

This, I say, is a great mystery, and deserves to be pried into by all the godly, both because much of the wisdom of heaven is discovered in it, and because the best saint is, or may be, concerned with it. Nor must we by any means let this truth be lost, because it is the truth; the text has declared it so, and to say otherwise is to belie the Word of God, to thwart the apostle, to soothe up hypocrites, to rob Christians of their privilege, and to take the glory from the head of Jesus Christ.[1]

The best saints are most sensible of their sins, and most apt to make mountains of their mole hills. Satan also, as has been already hinted, doth labour greatly to prevail with them to sin, and to provoke their God against them, by pleading what is true, or by surmising evilly of them, to the end they may be accused by him.[2] Great is his malice towards them, great is his diligence in seeking their destruction; wherefore greatly doth he desire to sift, to try, and winnow them, if perhaps he may work in their flesh to answer his design—that is, to break out in sinful acts, that he may have by law to accuse them to their God and Father. Wherefore, for their sakes this text abides, that they may see that, when they have sinned, "they have an Advocate with the Father, Jesus Christ the righteous." And thus have I showed you the nature, the order, and occasion of this office of our blessed Lord Jesus.

---

1 Luke 18:11–12.
2 Job 2:9.

HOW CHRIST MANAGES THE OFFICE OF AN ADVOCATE

SECONDLY, I come now *to show you how Jesus Christ doth manage this his office of an Advocate for us.* And that I may do this to your edification, I shall choose this method for the opening of it—*First.* Show you how he manages this office with his Father. *Second.* I shall show you how he manages it before him against our adversary.

First. How he manages this his office of Advocate with his Father.

1. He doth it by himself, by no other as deputy under him, no angel, no saint; no work has place here but Jesus, and Jesus only. This the text implies: "We have an Advocate;" speaking of one, but one, one alone; without an equal or an inferior. We have but one, and he is Jesus Christ. Nor is it for Christ's honour, nor for the honour of the law, or of the justice of God, that any but Jesus Christ should be an Advocate for a sinning saint. Besides, to assert the contrary, what doth it but lessen sin, and make the advocateship of Jesus Christ superfluous? It would lessen sin should it be removed by a saint or angel; it would make the advocateship of Jesus Christ superfluous, yea, needless, should it be possible that sin could be removed from us by either saint or angel.

Again; if God should admit of more advocates than one, and yet make mention of never an one but Jesus Christ; or if John should allow another, and yet speak nothing but of Jesus only; yea, that an advocate under that title should be mentioned but once, but once only in all the book of God, and yet that divers should be admitted, stands neither with the wisdom or love of God, nor with the faithfulness of the apostle. But saints have but one Advocate, if they will use him, or improve their faith in that office for their help, so; if not, they must take what follows. This I thought good to hint at, because the times are corrupt, and because ignorance and superstition always wait for a countenance with us, and these things have a natural tendency to darken all truth, so especially this, which bringeth to Jesus Christ so much glory, and yieldeth to the godly so much help and relief.

2. As Jesus Christ alone is Advocate, so God's bar, and that alone, is that before which he pleads for God is judge himself.[1] Nor can the cause which now he is to plead be removed into any other court, either by appeals or otherwise.

Could Satan remove us from heaven, to another court, he would certainly be too hard for us, because there we should want our Jesus, our Advocate, to plead our cause. Indeed, sometimes he impleads us before men, and they are glad of the occasion, for they and he are often one; but then we have leave to remove our cause, and to pray for a trial in the highest court, saying, "Let my sentence come forth from thy presence; let thine eyes behold the things that are equal."[2] This wicked world doth sentence us for our good deeds, but how then would they sentence us for our bad ones? But we will never appeal from heaven to earth for right, for here we have no Advocate; "our Advocate is with the Father, Jesus Christ the righteous."

3. As he pleadeth by himself alone, and nowhere else but in the court of heaven with the Father, so as he pleadeth with the Father for us, he observeth this rule—

(1.) He granteth and confesseth whatever can rightly be charged upon us; yet so as that he taketh the whole charge upon himself, acknowledging the crimes to be his own. "O God," says he, "thou knowest my foolishness, and my sins;" my guiltiness "is not hid from thee."[3] And this he must do, or else he can do nothing. If he hides the sin, or lesseneth it, he is faulty; if he leaves it still upon us, we die. He must, then, take our iniquity to himself, make it his own, and so deliver us; for having thus taken the sin upon himself, as lawfully he may, and lovingly doth, "for we are members of his body" ('tis his hand, 'tis his foot, 'tis his ear hath sinned), it followeth that we live if he lives; and who can desire more?[4] This, then, must be thoroughly

---

1 Deuteronomy 32:36; Hebrews 12:23.

2 Psalm 17:2.

3 Psalm 69:5.

4 This is the great mystery of godliness—God manifest in the flesh, making sinful creatures the members of his own body, and becoming a sin-offering

considered, if ever we will have comfort in a day of trouble and distress for sin.

And thus far there is, in some kind, a harmony betwixt his being a sacrifice, a priest, and an Advocate. As a sacrifice, our sins were laid upon him.[1] As a priest, he beareth them.[2] And as an Advocate, he acknowledges them to be his own.[3] Now, having acknowledged them to be his own, the quarrel is no more betwixt *us* and Satan, for the Lord Jesus has espoused our quarrel, and made it his. All, then, that we in this matter have to do, is to stand at the bar by faith among the angels, and see how the business goes. O blessed God! what a lover of mankind art thou! and how gracious is our Lord Jesus, in his thus managing matters for us.

(2.) The Lord Jesus having thus taken our sins upon himself, next pleads his own goodness to God on our behalf, saying, "Let not them that wait on thee, O Lord God of hosts, be ashamed for my sake: let not those that seek thee be confounded for my sake, O God of Israel: because for thy sake I have borne reproach; shame hath covered my face."[4] Mark, let them not be ashamed for my sake, let them not be confounded for my sake. Shame and confusion are the fruits of guilt, or of a charge for sin,[5] and are but an entrance into condemnation.[6] But behold how Christ pleads, saying, Let not that be for my sake, for the merit of my blood, for the perfection of my righteousness, for the prevalency of my intercession. Let them not be ashamed for my sake, O Lord God of hosts. And let no man object, because this text is in the Psalms, as if it were not spoken by the prophet of Christ; for both John and Paul, yea, and Christ himself, do make this psalm a prophecy of him. Compare verse 9 with John 2:17, and with Romans 15:3; and verse 21 with Matthew 27:48, and Mark 15:25. But is not this a wonderful thing, that Christ should first take our sins, and account them his own, and then

---

for them. It is a holy, a heavenly, a soul-comforting mystery, which should influence the Christian to an intense hatred to sin, as the cause of his Saviour's sufferings; and a still more intense love to him, who redeemed us at such a sacrifice.—(OFFOR.)

1 Isaiah 53.
2 Exodus 28:38.
3 Psalm 69:5.
4 Psalm 69:6–7.
5 Jeremiah 3:25.
6 Daniel 12:2; John 5:29.

plead the value and worth of his whole self for our deliverance? For by these words, "for my sake," he pleads his ownself, his whole self, and all that he is and has; and thus he put us in good estate again, though our cause was very bad.

To bring this down to weak capacities. Suppose a man should be indebted twenty thousand pounds, but has not twenty thousand farthings wherewith to pay; and suppose also that this man be arrested for this debt, and that the law also, by which he is sued, will not admit of a penny bate; this man may yet come well enough off, if his advocate or attorney will make the debt his own, and will, in the presence of the judges, out with his bags, and pay down every farthing. Why, this is the way of our Advocate. Our sins are called debts.[1] We are sued for them at the law.[2] And the devil is our accuser; but behold the Lord Jesus comes out with his worthiness, pleads it at the bar, making the debt his own.[3] And saith, Now let them not be ashamed for my sake, O Lord God of hosts: let them not be confounded for my sake, O God of Israel. And hence, as he is said to be an Advocate, so he is said to be a propitiation, or amends-maker, or one that appeaseth the justice of God for our sins—"If any man sin, we have an Advocate with the Father, Jesus Christ the righteous; and he is the propitiation for our sins."

And who can now object against the deliverance of the child of God? God cannot; for he, for Christ's sake, according as he pleaded, hath forgiven us all trespasses.[4] The devil cannot; his mouth is stopped, as is plain in the case of Joshua.[5] The law cannot; for that approveth of what Christ has done. This, then, is the way of Christ's pleading. You must know, that when Christ pleads with God, he pleads with a just and righteous God, and therefore he must plead law, and nothing but law; and this he pleaded in both these pleas—*First*, in confessing of the sin he justified the sentence of the law in pronouncing of it evil; and then in his laying of himself, his whole self, before God for that sin, he vindicated the sanction and perfection of the law. Thus, therefore, he magnifies the law, and makes it honourable, and yet brings off his client safe and sound in the view of all the angels of God.

---

1 Matthew 6:12.
2 Luke 12:59.
3 Mark 10:45; 2 Corinthians 3:5.
4 Colossians 2:13; Ephesians 4:32.
5 Zechariah 3.

(3.) The Lord Jesus having thus taken our sins upon himself, and presented God with all the worthiness that is in his whole self for them, in the next place he calleth for justice, or a just verdict upon the satisfaction he hath made to God and to his law. Then proclamation is made in open court, saying, "Take away the filthy garments from him," from him that hath offended, and clothe him with change of raiment.[1]

Thus the soul is preserved that hath sinned; thus the God of heaven is content that he should be saved; thus Satan is put to confusion, and Jesus applauded and cried up by the angels of heaven, and by the saints on earth. Thus have I showed you how Christ doth advocate it with God and his Father for us; and I have been the more particular in this, because the glory of Christ, and the comfort of the dejected, are greatly concerned and wrapt up in it. Look, then, to Jesus, if thou hast sinned; to Jesus, as an Advocate pleading with the Father for thee. Look to nothing else; for he can tell how, and that by himself, to deliver thee; yea, and will do it in a way of justice, which is a wonder; and to the shame of Satan, which will be his glory; and also to thy complete deliverance, which will be thy comfort and salvation.

Second, But to pass this and come to the second thing, which is, to show you how the Lord Jesus manages this his office of an Advocate before his Father against the adversary; for he pleadeth with the Father, but pleadeth against the devil; he pleadeth with the Father law and justice, but against the adversary he letteth out himself.

I say, as he pleads against the adversary, so he enlargeth himself with arguments over and besides those which he pleadeth with God his Father.

Nor is it meet or needful that our advocate, when he pleads against Satan, should so limit himself to matter of law, as when he pleadeth with his Father. The saint, by sinning, oweth Satan nothing; no law of his is broken thereby; why, then, should he plead for the saving of his people, justifying righteousness to him?

Christ, when he died, died not to satisfy Satan, but his Father; not to appease the devil, but to answer the demands of the justice of God; nor did he design, when he hanged on the tree, to triumph over his Father, but over Satan; "He redeemed

---
[1] Zechariah 3.

us," therefore, "from the curse of the law," by his blood.[1] And from the power of Satan, by his resurrection.[2] He delivered us from righteous judgment by price and purchase; but from the rage of hell by fight and conquest.

And as he acted thus diversely in the work of our redemption, even so he also doth in the execution of his Advocate's office. When he pleadeth with God, he pleadeth so; and when he pleadeth against Satan, he pleadeth so; and how he pleadeth with God when he dealeth with law and justice I have showed you. And now I will show you how he pleadeth before him against the "accuser of the brethren."

1. He pleads against him the well-pleasedness that his Father has in his merits, saying, This shall please the Lord, or this doth or will please the Lord, better than anything that can be propounded.[3] Now this plea being true, as it is, being established upon the liking of God Almighty; whatever Satan can say to obtain our everlasting destruction is without ground, and so unreasonable. "I am well pleased," saith God,[4] and again, "The Lord is well pleased for his (Christ's) righteousness' sake."[5] All that enter actions against others, pretend that wrong is done, either against themselves or against the king. Now Satan will never enter an action against us in the court above, for that wrong by us has been done to himself; he must pretend, then, that he sues us, for that wrong has, by us, been done to our king. But, behold, "We have an Advocate with the Father," and he has made compensation for our offences. He gave himself for our offences. But still Satan maintains his suit; and our God, saith Christ, is well pleased with us for this compensation-sake, yet he will not leave off his clamour. Come, then, says the Lord Jesus, the contention is not now against my people, but myself, and about the sufficiency of the amends that I have made for the transgressions of my people; but he is near that justifieth me, that approveth and accepteth of my doings, therefore shall I not be confounded. Who is mine adversary? let him come near me! Behold, "the Lord God will help me."[6] Who is he that condemneth me? Lo, they all shall, were

1 Galatians 3:13.
2 Hebrews 2:14.
3 Psalm 69:31.
4 Matthew 3:17.
5 Isaiah 42:21.
6 Isaiah 50:7–9.

there ten thousand times as many more of them, wax old as a garment; the moth shall eat them up. Wherefore, if the Father saith Amen to all this, as I have showed already that he hath and doth, the which also further appeareth, because the Lord God has called him the Saviour, the Deliverer, and the Amen; what follows, but that a rebuke should proceed from the throne against him? And this, indeed, our Advocate calls for from the hand of his Father, saying, O enemy, "the Lord rebuke thee;" yea, he doubles this request to the judge, to intimate his earnestness for such a conclusion, or to show that the enemy shall surely have it, both from our Advocate, and from him before whom Satan has so grievously accused us.[1]

For what can be expected to follow from such an issue in law as this is, but sound and severe snibs from the judge upon him that hath thus troubled his neighbour, and that hath, in the face of the country, cast contempt upon the highest act of mercy, justice, and righteousness, that ever the heavens beheld?[2] And all this is true with reference to the case in hand, wherefore, "The Lord rebuke thee," is that which, in conclusion, Satan must have for the reward of his works of malice against the children, and for his contemning of the works of the Son of God. Now, our Advocate having thus established, by the law of heaven, his plea with God for us against our accuser, there is way made for him to proceed upon a foundation that cannot be shaken; wherefore, he proceedeth in his plea, and further urges against this accuser of the brethren.

2. God's interest in this people; and prayeth that God would remember that: "The Lord rebuke thee, O Satan; the Lord that hath chosen Jerusalem, rebuke thee." True, the church, the saints, are despicable in the world; wherefore men do think to tread them down; the saints are, also, weak in grace, but have corruptions that are strong, and, therefore, Satan, the god of this world, doth think to tread them down; but the saints have a God, the living, the eternal God, and, therefore, they shall not be trodden down; yea, they "shall be holden up, for God is able to make them stand."[3]

It was Haman's mishap to be engaged against the queen,

---

1 Zechariah 3.
2 Altered, by a typographical error, in editions after the author's death, to "the heathens beheld."—(OFFOR.)
3 Romans 14:4.

and the kindred of the queen; it was that that made him he could not prosper; that brought him to contempt and the gallows. Had he sought to ruin another people, probably he might have brought his design to a desired conclusion; but his compassing the death of the queen spoiled all. Satan, also, when he fighteth against the church, must be sure to come to the worst, for God has a concern in that; therefore, it is said, "The gates of hell shall not prevail against it;" but this hindereth not but that he is permitted to make almost what spoils he will of those that belong not to God. Oh, how many doth he accuse, and soon get out from God, against them, a licence to destroy them! as he served Ahab, and many more. But this, I say, is a very great block in his way when he meddles with the children; God has an interest in them—"Hath God cast away his people? God forbid!"[1] The text intimates that they for sin had deserved it, and that Satan would fain have had it been so; but God's interest in them preserved them—"God hath not cast away his people, which he foreknew." Wherefore, when Satan accuseth them before God, Christ, as he pleadeth his own worth and merit, pleadeth also against him, that interest that God has in them.

And though this, to some, may seem but an indifferent plea; for what engagement lieth, may they say, upon God to be so much concerned with them, for they sin against him, and often provoke him most bitterly? Besides, in their best state, they are altogether vanity, and a very thing of nought—"What is man (sorry man), that thou art mindful of him," or that thou shouldest be so?

I answer, Though there lieth no engagement upon God for any worthiness that is in man, yet there lieth a great deal upon God for the worthiness that is in himself. God has engaged himself with his having chosen them to be a people to himself; and by this means they are so secured from all that all can do against them, that the apostle is bold, upon this very account, to challenge all despite to do its worst against them, saying, "Who shall lay anything to the charge of God's elect?"[2] Who? saith Satan; why, that will I. Ay, saith he, but who can do it, and prevail? "*It is* God that justifieth, who *is* he that condemneth?"[3] By which words the apostle clearly declareth that charges against

---

1 Romans 11:1–2.
2 Romans 8:33.
3 Romans 8:34.

the elect, though they may be brought against them, must needs prove ineffectual as to their condemnation; because their Lord God still will justify, for that Christ has died for them. Besides, a little to enlarge, the elect are bound to God by a sevenfold cord, and a threefold one is not quickly broken.

(1.) Election is eternal as God himself, and so without variableness or shadow of change, and hence it is called "an eternal purpose," and a "purpose of God" that must stand.[1]

(2.) Election is absolute, not conditional; and, therefore, cannot be overthrown by the sin of the man that is wrapt up therein. No works foreseen to be in us was the cause of God's choosing us; no sin in us shall frustrate or make election void— "Who shall lay anything to the charge of God's elect? *It is* God that justifieth."[2]

(3.) By the act of election the children are involved, wrapped up, and covered in Christ; he hath chosen us in him; not in ourselves, not in our virtues, no, not for or because of anything, but of his own will.[3]

(4.) Election includeth in it a permanent resolution of God to glorify his mercy on the vessels of mercy, thus foreordained unto glory.[4]

(5.) By the act of electing love, it is concluded that all things whatsoever shall work together for the good of them whose call to God is the fruit of this purpose, this eternal purpose of God.[5]

(6.) The eternal inheritance is by a covenant of free and unchangeable grace made over to those thus chosen; and to secure them from the fruits of sin, and from the malice of Satan, it is sealed by this our Advocate's blood, as he is Mediator of this covenant, who also is become surety to God for them; to wit, to see them forthcoming at the great day, and to set them then safe and sound before his Father's face after the judgment is over.[6]

(7.) By this choice, purpose, and decree, the elect, the concerned therein, have allotted them by God, and laid up for them, in Christ, a sufficiency of grace to bring them through all difficulties to glory; yea, and they, every one of them, after

---

1 Ephesians 3:11; Romans 9:11.
2 Romans 8:33; 9:11.
3 Ephesians 1:4–11.
4 Romans 9:15, 18, 23.
5 Romans 8:28–30.
6 Romans 9:23; Hebrews 7:22; 9:15, 17–24; 13:20; John 10:28–29.

the first act of faith—the which also they shall certainly attain, because wrapt up in the promise for them—are to receive the earnest and first fruits thereof into their souls.[1]

Now, put all these things together, and then feel if there be not weight in this plea of Christ against the devil. He pleads God's choice and interest in his saints against him—an interest that is secured by the wisdom of heaven, by the grace of heaven, by the power, will, and mercy of God, in Christ—an interest in which all the three Persons in the Godhead have engaged themselves, by mutual agreement and operation, to make good when Satan has done his all. I know there are some that object against this doctrine as false; but such, perhaps, are ignorant of some things else as well as of this. However, they object against the wisdom of God, whose truth it is, and against Christ our Advocate, whose argument, as he is such, it is; yea, they labour, what in them lieth, to wrest that weapon out of his hand, with which he so cudgelleth the enemy when, as Advocate, he pleadeth so effectually against him for the rescuing of us from the danger of judgment, saying, "The Lord rebuke thee, O Satan, even the Lord that hath chosen Jerusalem, rebuke thee."

Third. As Christ, as Advocate, pleads against Satan the interest that his Father hath in his chosen, so also he pleads against him by no less authority—his own interest in them. "Holy Father," saith he, "keep through thine own name those whom thou hast given me."[2] Keep them while in the world from the evil, the soul-damning evil of it. These words are directed to the Father, but they are levelled against the accusations of the enemy, and were spoken here to show what Christ will do for his, against our foe, when he is above. How, I say, he will urge before his Father his own interest in us against Satan, and against all his accusations, when he brings them to the bar of God's tribunal, with design to work our utter ruin. And is there not a great deal in it? As if Christ should say, Father, my people have an adversary who will accuse them for their faults before thee; but I will be their Advocate, and as I have bought them of thee, I will plead my right against him.[3] Our English proverb is, Interest will not lie; interest will make a

---
1 2 Timothy 1:9; Acts 14:22; Ephesians 1:4–5, 13–14.
2 John 17:11.
3 John 10:28.

man do that which otherwise he would not. How many thousands are there for whom Christ doth not so much as once open his mouth, but leaves them to the accusations of Satan, and to Ahab's judgment, nay, a worse, because there is none to plead their cause? And why doth he not concern himself with them? but because he is not interested in them—"I pray not for the world, but for them which thou hast given me, for they are thine; and all mine are thine, and I am glorified in them."[1]

Suppose so many cattle in such a pound, and one goes by whose they are not, doth he concern himself? No; he beholds them, and goes his way. But suppose that at his return he should find his own cattle in that pound, would he now carry it toward them as he did unto the other? No, no; he has interest here, they are his that are in the pound; now he is concerned, now he must know who put them there, and for what cause too they are served as they are; and if he finds them rightfully there, he will fetch them thence by ransom; but if wrongfully, he will replevy[2] them, and stand a trial at law with him that has thus illegally pounded his cattle. And thus it is betwixt Jesus Christ and his. He is interested in them; the cattle are his own, "his own sheep,"[3] but pounded by some other, by the law, or by the devil. If pounded by the law, he delivereth them by ransom; if pounded by the devil, he will replevy them, stand a trial at law for them, and will be, against their accuser, their Advocate himself. Nor can Satan withstand his plea, though he should against them join argument with the law; forasmuch, as has been proved before, he can and will, by what he has to produce and plead of his own, save his from all trespasses, charges, and accusations. Besides, all men know that a man's proper goods are not therefore forfeited, because they commit many, and them too great transgressions—"And if any man sin, we have an Advocate with the Father, Jesus Christ the righteous." Now, the strength of this plea thus grounded upon Christ's interest in his people is great, and hath many weighty reasons on its side; as—

1. They are mine; therefore in reason at my dispose, not at the dispose of an adversary; for while a thing can properly be

---

1 John 17:9–10.
2 Replevy—a form of law by which goods that are proved to have been wrongfully seized are re-delivered to the owner.—(Offor.)
3 John 10:3–4.

called mine, no man has therewith to do but myself; nor doth (a man, nor) Christ close his right to what he has by the weakness of that thing which is his proper right. He, therefore, as an Advocate, pleadeth interest, his own interest, in his people, and right must, with the Judge of all the earth, take place—"Shall not the Judge of all the earth do right?"[1]

2. They cost him dear; and that which is dear bought is not easily parted with.[2] They were bought with "his blood."[3] They were given him for his blood, and therefore, are "dear children;"[4] for they are his by the highest price; and this price he, as Advocate, pleadeth against the enemy of our salvation; yea, I will add, they are his, because he gave his all for them.[5] When a man shall give his all for this or that, then that which he so hath purchased is become his all. Now Christ has given his all for us; he made himself poor for us, wherefore we are become his all, his fulness; and so the church is called.[6] Nay, further, Christ likes well enough of his purchase, though it hath cost him his all—"The lines," says he, "are fallen to me in pleasant places; I have a goodly heritage."[7] Now, put all these things together, and there is a strong plea in them. Interest, such an interest, will not be easily parted with. But this is not all; for,

3. As they cost him dear, so he hath made them near to himself, near by way of relation. Now that which did not only cost dear, but that by way of relation is made so, that a man will plead heartily for. Said David to Abner, "Thou shalt not see my face except thou first bring Michal, Saul's daughter, when thou comest to see my face."[8] Saul's daughter cost me dear; I bought her with the jeopardy of my life; Saul's daughter is near to me; she is my beloved wife. He pleaded hard for her, because she was dear and near to him. Now, I say, the same is true in Christ; his people cost him dear, and he hath made them near unto him; wherefore, to plead interest in them, is to hold by an argument that is strong.

(a.) They are his spouse, and he hath made them so; they

---

1 Genesis 18:25.
2 1 Corinthians 6:20.
3 Ephesians 1:7; 1 Peter 1:18–19.
4 Ephesians 5:1.
5 2 Corinthians 8:9.
6 Ephesians 1:23.
7 Psalm 16.
8 2 Samuel 3:13–14.

are his love, his dove, his darling, and he accounts them so. Now, should a wretch attempt, in open court, to take a man's wife away from him, how would this cause the man to plead! Yea, and what judge that is just, and knows that the man has this interest in the woman pleaded for, would yield to, or give a verdict for the wretch, against the man whose wife the woman is? Thus Christ, in pleading interest—in pleading "thou gavest them me"—pleads by a strong argument, an argument that the enemy cannot invalidate. True, were Christ to plead this before a Saul,[1] or before Samson's wife's father, the Philistine,[2] perhaps such treacherous judges would give it against all right. But, I have told you, the court in which Christ pleads is the highest and the justest, and that from which there can be no appeal; wherefore Christ's cause, and so the cause of the children of God, must be tried before their Father, from whose face, to be sure, just judgment shall proceed. But,

(b.) As they are called his spouse, so they are called his flesh, and members of his body. Now, said Paul to the church, "Ye are the body of Christ, and members in particular."[3] This relation also makes a man plead hard. Were a man to plead for a limb, or a member of his own, how would he plead? what arguments would he use? and what sympathy and feeling would his arguments flow from? I cannot lose a hand, I cannot lose a foot, cannot lose a finger; why, saints are Christ's members, his members are of himself. With what strength of argument would a man plead the necessariness of his members to him, and the unnaturalness of his adversary in seeking the destruction of his members, and the deformity of his body! Yea, a man would shuck and cringe, and weep, and intreat, and make demurs, and halts, and delays, to a thousand years, if possible, before he would lose his members, or any one of them.

But, I say, how would he plead and advocate it for his members, if judge, and law, and reason, and equity, were all on his side, and if, by the adversary, there could be nothing urged, but that against which the Advocate had long before made provision for the effectual overthrow thereof? And all this is true as to the case that lies before us. Thus we see what strength there lieth in this second argument, that our Advocate bringeth for

---

[1] 1 Samuel 25:44.
[2] Judges 14:20.
[3] 1 Corinthians 12:27; Ephesians 5:30.

us against the enemy. They are his flesh and bones, his members; he cannot spare them; he cannot spare this, because, nor that, because, nor any, because, they are his members. As such, they are lovely to him; as such, they are useful to him; as such, they are an ornament to him; yea, though in themselves they are feeble, and through infirmity weak, much disabled from doing as they should. Thus, "If any man sin, we have an Advocate with the Father, Jesus Christ the righteous." But,

4. As Christ, as Advocate, pleads for us, against Satan, his Father's interest in us and his own; so he pleadeth against him that right and property that he hath in heaven, to give it to whom he will. He has a right to heaven as Priest and King; it is his also by inheritance; and since he will be so good a benefactor as to bestow this house on somebody, but not for their deserts, but not for their goodness, and since, again, he has to that end spilt his blood for, and taken a generation into covenant relation to him, that it might be bestowed on them; it shall be bestowed on them; and he will plead this, if there be need, if his people sin, and if their accuser seeks, by their sin, their ruin and destruction: "Father" saith he, "I will that they also, whom thou hast given me, be with me where I am; that they may behold my glory, which thou hast given me."[1] Christ's will is the will of heaven, the will of God. Shall not Christ, then, prevail?

"I will," saith Christ; "I will," saith Satan; but whose will shall stand? It is true, Christ in the text speaks more like an arbitrator than an Advocate; more like a judge than one pleading at a bar. I will have it so; I judge that so it ought to be, and must. But there is also something of plea in the words both before his Father, and against our enemy; and therefore he speaketh like one that can plead and determine also; yea, like one that has power so to do. But shall the will of heaven stoop to the will of hell? Or the will of Christ to the will of Satan? Or the will of righteousness to the will of sin? Shall Satan, who is God's enemy, and whose charge wherewith he chargeth us for sin, and which is grounded, not upon love to righteousness, but upon malice against God's designs of mercy, against the blood of Christ, and the salvation of his people—I say, shall this enemy and this charge prevail with God against the well-grounded plea of Christ, and against the salvation of God's elect, and so keep us out of heaven? No, no; Christ will have it otherwise,

---
1 John 17:24.

he is the great donator,[1] and his eye is good. True, Satan was turned out of heaven for that he sinned there, and we must be taken into heaven, though we have sinned here; this is the will of Christ, and, as Advocate, he pleads it against the face and accusation of our adversary. Thus, "If any man sin, we have an Advocate with the Father, Jesus Christ the righteous." But,

5. As Christ, as Advocate, pleadeth for us, against Satan, his Father's interest in us, and his own, and pleadeth also what right he has to dispose of the kingdom of heaven; so he pleadeth against this enemy, that malice and enmity that is in him, and upon which chiefly his charge against us is grounded, to the confusion of his face. This is evident from the title that our Advocate bestows upon him, while he pleads for us against him: "The Lord rebuke thee, O Satan," O enemy, saith he; for Satan is an enemy, and this name given him signifies so much. And lawyers, in their pleas, can make a great matter of such a circumstance as this; saying, My lord, we can prove that what is now pleaded against the prisoner at the bar is of mere malice and hatred, that has also a long time lain burning and raging in his enemy's breast against him. This, I say, will greatly weaken the plea and accusation of an enemy. But, says Jesus Christ, "Father, here is a plea brought in against my Joshua, that clothes him with filthy garments, but it is brought in against him by an enemy, by an enemy in the superlative or highest degree. One that hates goodness worse than he, and that loveth wickedness more than the man against whom at this time he has brought such a heinous charge." Then leaving with the Father the value of his blood for the accused, he turneth him to the accuser, and pleads against him as an enemy: "O Satan, thou that accusest my spouse, my love, my members, art SATAN, an enemy." But it will be objected, that the things charged are true. Grant it; yet what law takes notice of the plea of one who doth professedly act as an enemy? because it is not done of love to truth, and justice, and righteousness, nor intended for the honour of the king, nor for the good of the prosecuted; but to gratify malice and rage, and merely to kill and destroy. There is, therefore, a great deal of force and strength in an Advocate's pleading of such a circumstance against an accuser; especially when the crimes now charged are those, and only those for which

---

1 Donator—giver, donor; now obsolete.—(OFFOR.)

the law, in the due execution of it, has been satisfied before; wherefore now a lawyer has double and treble ground or matter to plead for his client against his enemy. And this advantage against him has Jesus Christ.

Besides, it is well known that Satan, as to us, is the original cause of those very crimes for which he accuses us at the bar of God's tribunal. Not to say anything of how he cometh to us, solicits us, tempts us, flatters us, and always, in a manner, lies at us to do those wicked things for which he so hotly pursues us to the bar of the judgment of God. For though it is not meet for us thus to plead,—to wit, laying that fault upon Satan, but rather upon ourselves,—yet our advocate will do it, and make work of it too before God. "Simon, Simon, behold, Satan hath desired *to have* you, that he might sift you as wheat; but I have prayed for thee, that thy faith fail not."[1] He maketh here mention of Satan's desires, by way of advantage against him; and, doubtless, so he did in his prayer with God for Peter's preservation. And what he did here, while on earth, as a Saviour in general, that he doth now in heaven as a Priest and an Advocate in special.

I will further suppose that which may be supposed, and that which is suitable to our purpose. Suppose, therefore, that a father that has a child whom he loveth, but the child has not half that wit that some of the family hath, and I am sure that we have less wit than angels; and suppose, also, that some bad-minded neighbour, by tampering with, tempting of, and by unwearied solicitations, should prevail with this child to steal something out of his father's house or grounds, and give it unto him; and this he doth on purpose to set the father against the child; and suppose, again, that it comes to the father's knowledge that the child, through the allurements of such an one, has done so and so against his father; will he therefore disinherit this child? Yea, suppose, again, that he that did tempt this child to steal, should be the first that should come to accuse this child to its father for so doing, would the father take notice of the accusation of such an one?—No, verily, we that are evil can do better than so; how then should we think that the God of heaven should do such a thing, since also we have a brother that is wise, and that will and can plead the very malice of our enemy that doth to us all these things against him

---
1 Luke 22:31–32.

for our advantage?—I say, this is the sum of this fifth plea of Christ our Advocate, against Satan. O Satan, says he, thou art an enemy to my people; thou pleadest not out of love to righteousness, not to reform, but to destroy my beloved and inheritance. The charge wherewith thou chargest my people is thine own.[1] Not only as to a matter of charge, but the things that thou accusest them of are thine, thine in the nature of them. Also, thou hast tempted, allured, flattered, and daily laboured with them, to do that for which now thou so willingly would have them destroyed. Yea, all this hast thou done of envy to my Father, and to godliness; of hatred to me and my people; and that thou mightest destroy others besides.[2] And now, what can this accuser say? Can he excuse himself? Can he contradict our Advocate? He cannot; he knows that he is a Satan, an enemy, and as an adversary has he sown his tares among the wheat, that it might be rooted up; but he shall not have his end; his malice has prevented[3] him, and so has the care and grace of our Advocate. The tares, therefore, he shall have returned unto him again; but the wheat, for all this, shall be gathered into God's barn.[4]

Thus, therefore, our Advocate makes use, in his plea against Satan, of the rage and malice that is the occasion of the enemy's charge wherewith he accuseth the children of God. Wherefore, when thou readest these words, "O Satan," say with thyself, Thus Christ our Advocate accuseth our adversary of malice and envy against God and goodness, while he accuseth us of the sins which we commit, for which we are sorry, and Christ has paid a price of redemption—"And (thus) if any man sin, we have an Advocate with the Father, Jesus Christ the righteous." But,

6. Christ, when he pleads as an Advocate for his people, in the presence of God against Satan, he can plead those very weaknesses of his people for which Satan would have them damned, for their relief and advantage. "*Is* not this a brand plucked out of the fire?" This is part of the plea of our Advocate against Satan for his servant Joshua, when he said, "The Lord

---

1 Job 8:4–6.
2 1 Chronicles 21:1.
3 Prevented—gone before, so as to be seen. "Let thy grace, O Lord, always prevent and follow us."—*Common Prayer.*—(OFFOR.)
4 Matthew 13:25–30.

rebuke thee, O Satan."[1] Now, to be a brand plucked out of the fire is to be a saint, impaired, weakened, defiled, and made imperfect by sin; for so also the apostle means when he saith, "And others save with fear, pulling *them* out of the fire; hating even the garment spotted by the flesh."[2] By fire, in both these places, we are to understand sin; for that it burns and consumes as fire.[3] Wherefore a man is said to burn when his lusts are strong upon him; and to burn in lusts to others, when his wicked heart runs wickedly after them.[4]

Also, when Abraham said, "I am but dust and ashes,"[5] he means, he was but what sin had left; yea, he had something of the smutch and besmearings of sin yet upon him. Wherefore it was a custom with Israel, in days of old, when they set days apart for confession of sin, and humiliation for the same, to sprinkle themselves with, or to wallow in dust and ashes, as a token that they did confess they were but what sin had left, and that they also were defiled, weakened, and polluted by it.[6]

This, then, is the next plea of our goodly Advocate for us: O Satan, this is "a brand plucked out of the fire." As who should say, Thou objected against my servant Joshua that he is black like a coal, or that the fire of sin at times is still burning in him. And what then? The reason why he is not totally extinct, as tow; is not thy pity, but my Father's mercy to him; I have plucked him out of the fire, yet not so out but that the smell thereof is yet upon him; and my Father and I, we consider his weakness, and pity him; for since he is as a brand pulled out, can it be expected by my Father or me that he should appear before us as clear, and do our biddings as well, as if he had never been there? This is "a brand plucked out of the fire," and must be considered as such, and must be borne with as such. Thus, as Mephibosheth pleaded for his excuse, his lameness,[7] so Christ pleads the infirm and indigent condition of his people, against Satan, for their advantage. Wherefore Christ, by such pleas as these for his people, doth yet further show the malice of Satan (for all this burning comes through him), yea, and by

---

1 Zechariah 3:2.
2 Jude 23.
3 Romans 1:27.
4 1 Corinthians 7:9.
5 Genesis 18:27.
6 Esther 4:1, 3; Jeremiah 6:26; Job 30:19; 42:6.
7 2 Samuel 19:24–26.

it he moveth the heart of God to pity us, and yet to be gentle, and long-suffering, and merciful to us; for pity and compassion are the fruits of the yearning of God's bowels towards us, while he considereth us as infirm and weak, and subject to slips, and stumbles, and falls, because of weakness.

And that Christ our Advocate, by thus pleading, doth turn things to our advantage, consider,

(1.) That God is careful, that through our weakness, our spirits do not fail before him when he chides.[1]

(2.) "He stayeth his rough wind in the day of the east wind," and debates about the measure of affliction, when, for sin, we should be chastened, lest we should sink thereunder.[2]

(3.) He will not strictly mark what is done amiss, because if he should, we cannot stand.[3]

(4.) When he threateneth to strike, his bowels are troubled, and his repentings are kindled together.[4]

(5.) He will spin out his patience to the utmost length, because he knows we are such bunglers at doing.[5]

(6.) He will accept of the *will* for the *deed,* because he knows that sin will make our best performances imperfect.[6]

(7.) He will count our little a very great deal, for that he knows we are so unable to do anything at all.[7]

(8.) He will excuse the *souls* of his people, and lay the fault upon their flesh, which has greatest affinity with Satan, if through weakness and infirmity we do not do as we should.[8] Now, as I said, all these things happen unto us, both infirmities and pity, because and for that we were once in the fire, and for that the weakness of sin abides upon us to this day. But none of this favour could come to us, nor could we, by any means, cause that our infirmities should work for us thus advantageously; but that Christ our Advocate stands our friend, and pleads for us as he doth.

But again, before I pass this over, I will, for the clearing of this, present you with a few more considerations, which are of

---

1 Isaiah 57:16–18.
2 Isaiah 27:7–9.
3 Psalm 130:3.
4 Hosea 11:8–9.
5 Jeremiah 9:24.
6 2 Corinthians 8:12.
7 Job 1:21.
8 Matthew 26:41; Romans 7.

another rank—to wit, that Christ our Advocate, as such, makes mention of our weaknesses so, against Satan, and before his Father, as to turn all to our advantage.

(1.) We are therefore to be saved by grace, because by reason of sin we are disabled from keeping of the law.[1]

(2.) We have given unto us the Spirit of grace to help, because we can do nothing that is good without it.[2]

(3.) God has put Christ's righteousness upon us to cover our nakedness with, because we have none of our own to do it withal.[3]

(4.) God alloweth us to ride in the bosom of Christ to the grave, and from thence in the bosom of angels to heaven, because our own legs are not able to carry us thither.[4]

(5.) God has made his Son our Head, our Priest, our Advocate, our Saviour, our Captain, that we may be delivered from all the infirmities and all the fiends that attend us, and that plot to do us hurt.[5]

(6.) God has put the fallen angels into chains,[6] that they might not follow us too fast, and has enlarged us,[7] and directed our feet in the way of his steps, that we may haste us to the strong tower and city of refuge for succour and safety, and has given good angels a charge to look to us.[8]

(7.) God has promised that we, at our counting days, shall be spared, "as a man spareth his own son that serveth him."[9]

Now, from all these things, it appears that we have indulgence at God's hand, and that our weaknesses, as our Christ manages the matter for us, are so far off from laying a block or bar in the way to the enjoyment of favour, that they also work for our good; yea, and God's foresight of them has so kindled his bowels and compassion to us, as to put him upon devising of such things for our relief, which by no means could have been, had not sin been with us in the world, and had not the best of saints been "as a brand plucked out of the burning."

---

1 Deuteronomy 9:5; Isaiah 64:6.
2 Ephesians 2:5; Romans 8:26.
3 Philippians 3:7–8; Ezekiel 16:8.
4 Isaiah 40:11; 46:4; Psalm 48:14; Luke 16:22.
5 Ephesians 1:22; Colossians 1:18; Hebrews 7:21.
6 2 Peter 2:4; Revelation 20:1–2.
7 Psalm 4:1.
8 Hebrews 1:14; Psalm 34:7.
9 Malachi 3:17.

I have seen men (and yet they are worse than God) take most care of, and, also, best provide for, those of their children that have been most infirm and helpless;[1] and our Advocate "shall gather his lambs with his arms, and carry *them* in his bosom;" yea, and I know that there is such an art in showing and making mention of weaknesses as shall make the tears stand in a parent's eyes, and as shall make him search to the bottom of his purse to find out what may do his weakling good. Christ, also, has that excellent art, as he is an Advocate with the Father for us; he can so make mention of us and of our infirmities, while he pleads before God, against the devil, for us, that he can make the bowels of the Almighty yearn towards us, and to wrap us up in their compassions. You read much of the pity, compassion, and of the yearning of the bowels of the mighty God towards his people; all which, I think, is kindled and made burn towards us, by the pleading of our Advocate. I have seen fathers offended with their children; but when a brother had turned a skilful advocate, the anger has been appeased, and the means have been concealed. We read but little of this Advocate's office of Jesus Christ, yet much of the fruit of it is extended to the churches; but as the cause of smiles, after offences committed, is made manifest afterwards, so at the day when God will open all things, we shall see how many times our Lord, as an Advocate, pleaded for us, and redeemed us by his so pleading, into the enjoyments of smiles and embraces, who, for sin, but a while before, were under frowns and chastisements. And thus much for the making out how Christ doth manage his office of being an Advocate for us with the Father—"If any man sin, we have an Advocate with the Father, Jesus Christ the righteous."

---

1 This may refer to Bunyan's own feelings, which are so passionately expressed in his *Grace Abounding*, No. 327, when he was dragged from his home, his wife, and his children, to be shut up in Bedford jail, for obedience to God. He exclaims, "My poor *blind* child, who lay *nearer* my heart than all I had besides, thou must be beaten, must beg, suffer hunger, cold, nakedness, and a thousand calamities, though I cannot now endure that the wind should blow upon thee. I thought this would break my heart to pieces."—(Offor.)

WHO HAVE CHRIST FOR AN ADVOCATE

THIRDLY, And I shall come now to the third head; *to wit, to show you more particularly who they are that have Jesus Christ for their Advocate.*

In my handling of this head, I shall show, *First,* That this office of an advocate differeth from that of a priest, and how. *Second,* I shall show you how far Christ extendeth this his office of advocateship—I mean, in matters concerning the people of God. And then, *Third,* I shall come more directly to show who they are that have Christ for their Advocate.

First, For the first of these, That this office of Christ, as an Advocate, differeth from that of a Priest. That he is a Priest, a Priest for ever, I heartily acknowledge; but that his priesthood and advocateship should be one and the self-same office, I cannot believe.

1. Because they differ in name. We may as well say a father, as such, is a son, or that father and son is the self-same relation, as say a priest and an advocate, as to office, are but one and the same thing. They differ in name as much as priest and sacrifice do: a priest is one, and a sacrifice is another; and though Christ is Priest and Sacrifice too, yet, as a Priest, he is not a Sacrifice, nor, as a Sacrifice, a Priest.

2. As they differ in name, so they differ in the nature of office. A priest is to slay a sacrifice; an advocate is to plead a cause; a priest is to offer his sacrifice, to the end that, by the merit thereof, he may appease; an advocate is to plead, to plead according to law; a priest is to make intercession, by virtue of his sacrifice; an advocate is to plead law, because amends is made.

3. As they differ in name and nature, so they also differ as to their extent. The priesthood of Christ extendeth itself to the

whole of God's elect, whether called or in their sins; but Christ, as Advocate, pleadeth only for the children.

4. As they differ in name, in nature, and extent, so they differ as to the persons with whom they have to do. We read not anywhere that Christ, as Priest, has to do with the devil as an antagonist, but, as an Advocate, he hath.

5. As they differ in these, so they differ as to the matters about which they are employed. Christ, as Priest, concerns himself with every wry thought, and, also, with the least imperfection or infirmity that attends our most holy things; but Christ, as Advocate, doth not so, as I have already showed.

6. So that Christ, as Priest, goes before, and Christ, as an Advocate, comes after; Christ, as Priest, continually intercedes; Christ, as Advocate, in case of great transgressions, pleads: Christ, as Priest, has need to act always, but Christ, as Advocate, sometimes only. Christ, as Priest, acts in times of peace; but Christ, as Advocate, in times of broils, turmoils, and sharp contentions; wherefore, Christ, as Advocate, is, as I may call him, a reserve, and his time is then to arise, to stand up and plead, when HIS are clothed with some filthy sin that of late they have fallen into, as David, Joshua, or Peter. When some such thing is committed by them, as ministereth to the enemy a show of ground to question the truth of their grace; or when it is a question, and to be debated, whether it can stand with the laws of heaven, with the merits of Christ, and the honour of God, that such a one should be saved. Now let an advocate come forth, now let him have time to plead, for this is a fit occasion for the saints' Advocate to stand up to plead for the salvation of his people. But,

Second, I come next to show you how far this office of an Advocate is extended. I hinted at this before, so now shall be the more brief.

1. By this office he offereth no sacrifice; he only, as to matter of justice, pleads the sacrifice offered.

2. By this office he obtains the conversion of none; he only thereby secureth the converted from the damnation which their adversary, for sins after light and profession, endeavoureth to bring them to.

3. By this office he prevents not temporal punishment, but by it he chiefly preserveth the soul from hell.

4. By this office he brings in no justifying righteousness

for us, he only thereby prevaileth to have the dispose of that brought in by himself, as Priest, for the justifying of those, by a new and fresh act, who had made their justification doubtful by new falls into sin. And this is plain in the history of our Joshua, so often mentioned before.[1]

5. As Priest, he hath obtained eternal redemption for us; and as Advocate, he by law, maintaineth our right thereto, against the devil and his angels.

Third, I come now to show you who they are that have Jesus Christ for their Advocate. And this I shall do—first, more generally, and then shall be more particular and distinct about it.

1. More generally. *They are all the truly gracious; those that are the children by adoption*; and this the text affirmeth—"My little children, these things write I unto you, that ye sin not. And if any man sin, we have an Advocate with the Father, Jesus Christ the righteous." They are, then, the children, by adoption, that are the persons concerned in the advocateship of Jesus Christ. The priesthood of Christ extendeth itself to the whole body of the elect, but the advocateship of Christ doth not so. This is further cleared by this apostle; and in this very text, if you consider what immediately follows—"We have an Advocate," says he, "and he is the propitiation for our sins." He is our Advocate, and also our Priest. As an Advocate, ours only; but as a propitiation, not ours only, but also for the sins of the whole world; to be sure, for the elect throughout the world, and they that will extend it further, let them.

And I say again, had he not intended that there should have been a straiter limit put to the Advocateship of Christ than he would have us put to his priestly office, what needed he, when he speaketh of the propitiation which relates to Christ as Priest, have added—"And not for ours only?" As an Advocate, then, he engageth for us that are children; and as a Priest, too, he hath appeased God's wrath for our sins; but as an Advocate his offices are confined to the children only, but as a Priest he is not so. He is the propitiation for our sins, and not for ours only. The sense, therefore, of the apostle should, I think, be this— That Christ, as a Priest, hath offered a propitiatory sacrifice for all; but as an Advocate he pleadeth only for the children. Children, we have an Advocate to ourselves, and he is also our Priest; but as he is a Priest, he is not ours only, but maketh, as

---
1 Zechariah 3.

such, amends for all that shall be saved. The elect, therefore, have the Lord Jesus for their Advocate then, and then only, when they are by calling put among the children; because, as Advocate, he is peculiarly the children's—"My little children, WE have an Advocate,"

Objection. But he also saith, "If any man sin, we have an Advocate;" any man that sinneth seems, by the text, notwithstanding what you say, "to have an Advocate with the Father."

Answer. By any man, must not be meant any of the world, nor any of the elect, but any man in faith and grace; for he still limits this general term, "any man," with this restriction, "we"—Children, "if any man sin, we have an Advocate." WE, any man of us. And this is yet further made appear, since he saith that it is to them he writes, not only here, but further in this chapter—"I write unto YOU, little children; I write unto you, fathers; I write unto you, young men."[1] These are the persons intended in the text, for under these three heads are comprehended all men; for they are either children, and so men in nature, or young men, and so men in strength; or else they are fathers, and so aged, and of experience. Add to this, by "any man," that the apostle intendeth not to enlarge himself beyond the persons that are in grace; but to supply what was wanting by that term "little children;" for since the strongest saint may have need of an Advocate, as well as the most feeble of the flock, why should the apostle leave it to be so understood as if the children, and the children only, had an interest in that office? Wherefore, after he had said, "My little children, I write unto you, that ye sin not;" he then adds, with enlargement, "If any man sin, we have an Advocate with the Father." Yet the little children may well be mentioned first, since they most want the knowledge of it, are most feeble, and so by sin may be forced most frequently to act faith on Christ, as Advocate. Besides, they are most ready, through temptation, to question whether they have so good a right to Christ in all his offices as have better and more well-grown saints; and, therefore, they, in this the apostle's salutation, are first set down in the catalogue of names—"My little children, I write unto you, that ye sin not. If any man sin, we have an Advocate with the Father, Jesus Christ the righteous." So, then, the children of God are they who have the Lord Jesus, an Advocate for them with the

---

1 1 John 2:12–13.

Father. The least and biggest, the oldest and youngest, the feeblest and the strongest; ALL the children have an Advocate with the Father, Jesus Christ the righteous.

(1.) Since, then, the children have Christ for their advocate, art thou a child? Art thou begotten of God by his Word?[1] Hast thou in thee the spirit of adoption?[2] Canst thou in faith say, Father, Father, to God? Then is Christ thy Advocate, thine Advocate, "now to appear in the presence of God for thee."[3] To appear there, and to plead there, in the face of the court of heaven, for thee; to plead there against thine adversary, whose accusations are dreadful, whose subtilty is great, whose malice is inconceivable, and whose rage is intolerable; to plead there before a just God, a righteous God, a sin-revenging God: before whose face thou wouldst die if thou wast to show thyself, and at his bar to plead thine own cause. But,

(2.) There is a difference in children; some are bigger than some; there are children and little children—"My little children, I write unto you." Little children; some of the little children can neither say Father, nor so much as know that they themselves are children.

This is true in nature, and so it is in grace; wherefore, notwithstanding what was said under the first head, it doth not follow, that if I be a child I must certainly know it, and also be able to call God, Father. Let the first, then, serve to poise and balance the confident ones, and let this be for the relief of those more feeble; for they that are children, whether they know it or no, have Jesus Christ for their Advocate, for Christ is assigned to be our Advocate by the Judge, by the King, by our God and Father, although we have not known it. True, at present, there can come from hence, to them that are thus concerned in the advocateship of Christ, but little comfort; but yet it yields them great security; they have "an Advocate with the Father, Jesus Christ the righteous." God knows this, the devil feels this, and the children shall have the comfort of it afterwards. I say, the time is coming when they shall know that even then, when they knew it not, they had an Advocate with the Father; an Advocate who was neither loath, nor afraid, nor ashamed, to plead for their defence against their proudest foe. And will not

---

1 James 1:18.
2 Galatians 4:6.
3 Hebrews 9:24.

this, when they know it, yield them comfort? Doubtless it will; yea, more, and of a better kind, than that which flows from the knowledge that one is born to crowns and kingdoms.

Again; as he is an Advocate for the children, so he is also, as before was hinted, for the strong and experienced; for no strength in this world secureth from the rage of hell; nor can any experience, while we are here, fortify us against his assaults. There is also an incidency in the best to sin; and the bigger man, the bigger fall; for the more hurt, and the greater damage. Wherefore it is of absolute necessity that an advocate be provided for the strong as for the weak. "Any man;" he that is most holy, most reformed, most refined, and most purified, may as soon be in the dirt as the weakest Christian; and, so far as I can see, Satan's design is against them most. I am sure the greatest sins have been committed by the biggest saints. This wayfaring man came to David's house, and when he stood up against Israel, he provoked David to number the people.[1] Wherefore they have as much need of an advocate as have the youngest and most feeble of the flock. What a mind had he to try a fall with Peter! and how quickly did he break the neck of Judas! The like, without doubt, he had done to Peter, had not Jesus, by stepping in, prevented. As long as sin is in our flesh, there is danger. Indeed, he saith of the young men that they are strong, and that they have overcome the wicked one; but he doth not say they have *killed* him. As long as the devil is alive there is danger; and though a strong Christian may be too hard for, and may overcome him in one thing, he may be too hard for, yea, and may overcome him two for one afterwards. Thus he served David, and thus he served Peter, and thus he, in our day, has served many more. The strongest are weak, the wisest are fools, when suffered to be sifted as wheat in Satan's sieve; yea, and have often been so proved, to the wounding of their great hearts, and the dishonour of religion. To conclude this: God of his mercy hath sufficiently declared the truth of what I say, by preparing for the best, the strongest, and most sanctified, as well as for the least, weakest, and most feeble saint, an Advocate—"My little children, I write unto you, that ye sin not. And if any man sin, we have an Advocate with the Father, Jesus Christ the righteous."

2. But some may object, that what has been said as to

---

[1] 2 Samuel 12:4, 7; 1 Chronicles 21:1.

discovering for whom Christ is an Advocate has been too general, and, therefore, would have me come more to particulars, else they can get no comfort. Well, inquiring soul, so I will; and, therefore, hearken to what I say.

(1.) Wouldest thou know whether Christ is thine Advocate or no? I ask, *Hast thou entertained him* so to to be? When men have suits of law depending in any of the king's courts above, they entertain their attorney or advocate to plead their cause, and so he pleads for them. I say, hast thou entertained Jesus Christ for thy lawyer to plead thy cause? "Plead *my cause*, O Lord," said David,[1] and again, "Judge me, O God, and plead my cause."[2] This, therefore, is the first thing that I would propound to thee: Hast thou, with David, entertained him for thy lawyer, or, with good Hezekiah, cried out, "O Lord, I am oppressed; undertake for me."[3] What sayest thou, soul? Hast thou been with him, and prayed him to plead thy cause, and cried unto him to undertake for thee? This I call entertaining of him to be thy advocate, and I choose to follow the similitude, both because the Scripture seems to smile upon such a way of discourse, and because thy question doth naturally lead me to it. Wherefore, I ask again, hast thou been with him? Hast thou entertained him? Hast thou desired him to plead thy cause?

Question. Thou wilt say unto me, How should I know that I have done so?

Answer. I answer, Art thou sensible that thou hast an action commenced against thee in that high court of justice that is above? I say, Art thou sensible of this? For the defendants—and all God's people are defendants—do not use to entertain their lawyers, but from knowledge, that an action either is, or may be, commenced against them before the God of heaven. If thou sayest yea, then I ask, Who told thee that thou standest accused for transgression before the judgment-seat of God? I say, Who told thee so? Hath the Holy Ghost, hath the world, or hath thy conscience? For nothing else, as I know of, can bring such tidings to thy soul.

Again; Hast thou found a failure in all others that might have been entertained to plead thy cause? Some make their sighs, their tears, their prayers, and their reformations, their

---

1 Psalm 35:1.
2 Psalm 43:1.
3 Isaiah 38:14.

advocates—"Hast thou tried these, and found them wanting?" Hast thou seen thy state to be desperate, if the Lord Jesus doth not undertake to plead thy cause? for Jesus is not entertained so long as men can make shift without him. But when it comes to this point I perish for ever, notwithstanding the help of all, if the Lord Jesus steps not in. Then Lord Jesus, Lord Jesus, good Lord Jesus! undertake for me. Hast thou therefore been with Jesus Christ as concerned in thy soul, as heartily concerned about the action that thou perceivest to be commenced against thee?

Question. You will say, How should I know that?

Answer. I answer, Hast thou well considered the nature of the crime wherewith thou standest charged at the bar of God? Hast thou also considered the justness of the Judge? Again I ask, Hast thou considered what truth, as to matter of fact, there is in the things whereof thou standest accused? Also, Hast thou considered the cunning, the malice, and diligence of thy adversary, with the greatness of the loss thou art like to sustain, shouldst thou with Ahab, in the book of Kings,[1] or with the hypocrites in Isaiah,[2] have the verdict of the Lord God go out from the throne against thee? I ask thee these questions, because if thou art in the knowledge of these things to seek, or if thou art not deeply concerned about the greatness of the damage that will certainly overtake thee, and that for ever, shouldest thou be indeed accused before God, and have none to plead thy cause, thou hast not, nor canst not, let what will come upon thee, have been with Jesus Christ to plead thy cause; and so, let thy case be never so desperate, thou standest alone, and hast no helper.[3] Or if thou hast, they, not being the advocate of God's appointing, must needs fall with thee, and with thy burden. Wherefore, consider of this seriously, and return thy answer to God, who can tell if truth shall be found in thy answers, better by far than any; for it is he that tries the reins and the heart, and therefore to him I refer thee. But,

(2.) Wouldst thou know whether Jesus Christ is thine advocate? Then I ask again, *Hast thou revealed thy cause unto him?*—I say, Hast thou revealed thy cause unto him? For he that goeth to law for his right, must not only go to a lawyer,

---

1 1 Kings 22:17–23.
2 Isaiah 6:5–10.
3 Job 30:13; 9:13.

and say, Sir, I am in trouble, and am to have a trial at law with mine enemy, pray undertake my cause; but he must also reveal to his lawyer his cause. He must go to him and tell him what is the matter, how things stand, where the shoe pinches, and so. Thus did the church of old, and thus doth every true Christian now; for though nothing can be hid from him, yet he will have things out of thine own mouth; he will have thee to reveal thy matters unto him.[1] "O Lord of hosts," said Jeremiah, "that judgest righteously, that triest the reins and the heart, let me see thy vengeance on them: for unto thee have I revealed my cause."[2] And again; "But, O Lord of hosts, that triest the righteous, *and* seest the reins and the heart, let me see thy vengeance on them; for unto thee have I opened my cause."[3] Seest thou here, how saints of old were wont to do? how they did, not only in a general way, entreat Christ to plead their cause, but in a particular way, go to him and reveal, or open their cause unto him?

O! it is excellent to behold how some sinners will do this when they get Christ and themselves in a closet alone; when they, upon their bare knees, are pouring out of their souls before him; or, like the woman in the gospel, telling him all the truth.[4] O! saith the soul, Lord, I am come to thee upon an earnest business; I am arrested by Satan; the bailiff was mine own conscience, and I am like to be accused before the judgment-seat of God. My salvation lies at stake; I am questioned for my interest in heaven; I am afraid of the Judge; my heart condemns me.[5] Mine enemy is subtle, and wanteth not malice to prosecute me to death, and then to hell. Also, Lord, I am sensible that the law is against me, for indeed I have horribly sinned, and thus and thus have I done. Here I lie open to law, and there I lie open to law; here I have given the adversary advantage, and there he will surely have a hank[6] against me. Lord, I am distressed, undertake for me! And there are some things that thou must be acquainted with about thine Advocate, before thou wilt venture to go thus far with him. As,

(*a*.) Thou must know him to be a friend, and not an enemy,

---
1 Matthew 20:32.
2 Jeremiah 11:20.
3 Jeremiah 20:12.
4 Mark 5.
5 1 John 3:20.
6 A hank—a check, an influence over; obsolete.—(Offor.)

unto whom thou openest thy heart; and until thou comest to know that Christ is a friend to thee, or to souls in thy condition, thou wilt never reveal thy cause unto him, not thy whole cause unto him. And it is from this that so many that have soul causes hourly depending before the throne of God, and that are in danger every day of eternal damnation, forbear to entertain Jesus Christ for their Advocate, and so wickedly conceal their matters from him; but "he that hideth his sins shall not prosper."[1,2] This, therefore, must first be believed by thee before thou wilt reveal thy cause unto him.

(b.) A man, when his estate is called in question, I mean his right and title thereto, will be very cautious, especially if he also questions his title to it himself, unto whom he reveals that affair; he must know him to be one that is not only friendly, but faithful, to whom he reveals such a secret as this. Why, thus it is with Christ and the soul. If the soul is not somewhat persuaded of the faithfulness of Christ—to wit, that if he can do him no good, he will do him no harm, he will never reveal his cause unto him, but will seek to hide his counsel from the Lord. This, therefore, is another thing by which thou mayest know that thou hast Christ for thine Advocate, if thou hast heartily and in very deed revealed thy cause unto him. Now, they that do honestly reveal their cause to their lawyer, will endeavour to possess him, as I hinted before, with the worst; they will, with words, make it as bad as they may; for, think they, by that means I shall prepare him for the worst that mine enemy can do. And thus souls deal with Jesus Christ;[3] with several others that might be named, and see if God's people have not done so. "I said," saith David, "I will confess my transgressions unto the Lord; and thou forgavest the iniquity of my sin." But,

(3.) Hast thou Jesus Christ for thine Advocate? or wouldst thou know if thou hast? Then I ask again, *Hast thou committed thy cause to him?* When a man entertains[4] his lawyer to stand for him and to plead his cause, he doth not only reveal, but commit his cause unto him. "I would seek unto God," says

---

1 Proverbs 28:13.
2 Quoted from the Genevan, or Puritan translation.—(OFFOR.)
3 See Psalm 51 and Psalm 38.
4 Entertains his lawyer—hires or retains. So Shakespeare—
"Sweet lady, entertain him,
To be my fellow-servant to your ladyship."
Gentleman of Verona, Scene IV.—(OFFOR.)

Eliphaz to Job, "and unto God would I commit my cause."[1] Now there is a difference betwixt revealing my cause and committing of it to a man. To reveal my cause is to open it to one; and to commit it to him is to trust it in his hand. Many a man will reveal his cause to him unto whom he will yet be afraid to commit it; but now, he that entertains a lawyer to plead his cause, doth not only reveal but commit his cause unto him. As, suppose right to his estate be called in question; why, then, he not only reveals his cause to his lawyer, but puts into his hands his evidences, deeds, leases, mortgages, bonds, or what else he hath, to show a title to his estate by. And thus doth Christians deal with Christ; they deliver up all unto him—to wit, all their signs, evidences, promises, and assurances, which they have thought they had for heaven and the salvation of their souls, and have desired him to peruse, to search, and try them every one. "And see if *there be any* wicked way in me, and lead me in the way everlasting."[2] This is committing of thy cause to Christ, and this is the hardest task of all, for the man that doth thus, he trusteth Christ with all; and it implieth, that he will live and die, stand and fall, lose and win, according as Christ will manage his business. Thus did Paul,[3] and thus Peter admonishes us to do. Now he that doth this must be convinced,

(*a*.) Of the ability of Jesus Christ to defend him; for a man will not commit so great a concern as his all is to his friend. No; not to his friend, be he never so faithful, if he perceives not in him ability to save him, and to preserve what he hath, against all the cavils of an enemy. And hence it is that the ability of Jesus Christ, as to the saving of his people, is so much insisted on in the Scripture; as, "I have laid help upon *one that is* mighty."[4] "I that speak in righteousness, mighty to save."[5] And again, "He shall send them a Saviour, and a great one."[6]

(*b*.) As they must be convinced of his ability to help them, so they must of his courage; a man that has parts sufficient may yet fail his friend for want of courage; wherefore, the courage and greatness of Christ's Spirit, as to his undertaking of the cause of his people, is also amply set out in Scripture. "He shall

---

1 Job 5:8.
2 Psalm 139:23–24.
3 2 Timothy 1:12.
4 Psalm 89:19.
5 Isaiah 63:1.
6 Isaiah 19:20.

not fail nor be discouraged, till he have set judgment in the earth," "till he send forth judgment unto victory."¹

(*c.*) They must also be convinced of his willingness to do this for them; for though one be able and of courage sufficient, yet if he is not willing to undertake one's cause, what is it the better? Wherefore, he declareth his willingness also, and how ready he is to stand up to plead the cause of the poor and of them that are in want. "The Lord will plead their cause, and spoil the soul of those that spoiled them."²

(*d.*) They must also be convinced of this—that Christ is tender, and will not be offended at the dulness of his client. Some men can reveal their cause to their lawyers better than some, and are more serviceable and handy in that affair than others. But, saith the Christian, I am dull and stupid that way, will not Christ be shuff³ and shy with me because of this? Honest heart! He hath a supply of thy defects⁴ in himself, and knoweth what thou wantest, and where the shoe pinches, though thou art not able distinctly to open matters to him. The child is pricked with a pin, and lies crying in the mother's lap, but cannot show its mother where the pin is; but there is pity enough in the mother to supply this defect of the child; wherefore she undresses it, opens it, searches every clout from head to the foot of the child, and so finds where the pin is. Thus will thy lawyer do; he will search and find out thy difficulties, and where Satan seeketh an advantage of thee, accordingly will provide his remedy.

(*e.*) O, but will he not be weary? The prophet complains of some, "that they weary God."⁵ And mine is a very cross and intricate cause; I have wearied many a good man while I have been telling my tale unto him, and I am afraid that I shall also weary Jesus Christ. *Answer.* Soul, he suffered and did bear with the manners of Israel forty years in the wilderness; and hast thou tried him half so long?⁶ The good souls that have gone before thee have found him "a tried stone," a sure one to be trusted to as to this,⁷ And the prophet saith positively

---

1 Isaiah 42:4; Matthew 12:20.
2 Proverbs 22:23.
3 Shuff—from the old Saxon word *schufan*, to reject, cast away.—(Offor.)
4 Supply of thy defects—a sufficiency in himself to supply all thy defects and deficiencies.—(Offor.)
5 Isaiah 7:13.
6 Acts 13:18.
7 Isaiah 28:16.

that "he fainteth not, neither is weary;" and that "there is no searching of his understanding."[1] Let all these things prevail with thee to believe, that if thou hast committed thy cause unto him, he will bring it to pass, to a good pass, to so good a pass as will glorify God, honour Christ, save thee, and shame the devil. But,

(4.) Wouldst thou know whether Jesus Christ is thine Advocate, whether he has taken in hand to plead thy cause? Then, I ask, *dost thou*, together with what has been mentioned before, *wait upon him according to his counsel, until things shall come to a legal issue?* Thus must clients do. There is a great many turnings and windings about suits and trials at law; the enemy, also, with his supersedeas,[2] cavils, and motions, often defers a speedy issue; wherefore, the man whose is the concern must wait; as the prophet said, "I will look," said he, "unto the Lord; I will wait for the God of my salvation." But how long, prophet, wilt thou wait? Why, says he, "until he plead my cause, and execute judgment for me."[3]

Perhaps when thy cause is tried, things for the present are upon this issue; thy adversary, indeed, is cast, but whether thou shalt have an absolute discharge, as Peter had, or a conditional one, as David, and as the Corinthians had, that is the question.[4] True, thou shalt be completely saved at last; but yet whether it is not best to leave to thee a memento of God's displeasure against thy sin, by awarding that the sword shall never depart from thy house, or that some sore sickness or other distresses shall haunt thee as long as thou livest, or, perhaps, that thou shalt walk without the light of God's countenance for several years and a day. Now, if any of these three things happen unto thee, thou must exercise patience, and wait; thus did David—"I waited patiently;" and again he exercises his soul in this virtue, saying "My soul, wait thou only upon God; for my expectation *is* from him."[5] For now we are judged of the Lord,

---

1 Isaiah 40:28.
2 Supersedeas—a writ to stay proceedings, for reasons expressed in it. "Cavils and motions;" quibbles or quirks of special pleading, and moving a court of law to occasion delay and weary out an honest suitor; much of this nuisance has been abated, but enough remains to render a lawsuit uncertain, vexatious, tedious, and expensive.—(Offor.)
3 Micah 7:7–10.
4 2 Samuel 12:10–14.
5 Psalm 62:5.

that we may not be condemned with the world. And by this judgment, though it sets us free from their damnation, yet we are involved in many troubles, and, perhaps, must wait many a day before we can know that, as to the main, the verdict hath gone on our side. Thus, therefore, in order to thy waiting upon him without fainting, it is meet that thou shouldest know the methods of him that manages thy cause for thee in heaven; and suffer not mistrust to break in and bear sway in thy soul, for "he will" at length "bring thee forth to the light, *and* thou shalt behold his righteousness. *She, also, that is* thine enemy shall see *it*, and shame shall cover her which said unto thee, Where is the Lord thy God?"[1]

Question. But what is it to wait upon him according to his counsel?

Answer. (*a.*) To wait is to be of good courage, to live in expectation, and to look for deliverance, though thou hast sinned against thy God. "Wait on the Lord, be of good courage, and he shall strengthen thine heart; wait, I say, on the Lord."[2]

(*b.*) To wait upon him is to keep his way, to walk humbly in his appointments. "Wait on the Lord, and keep his way, and he shall exalt thee to inherit the land."[3]

(*c.*) To wait upon him is to observe and keep those directions which he giveth thee; to observe even while he stands up to plead thy cause; for without this, or not doing this, a man may mar his cause in the hand of him that is to plead it; wherefore, keep thee far from an evil matter, have no correspondence with thine enemy, walk humbly for the wickedness thou hast committed, and loathe and abhor thyself for it, in dust and ashes. To these things doth the Scripture everywhere direct us.

(*d.*) To wait, is also to incline, to hearken to those further directions which thou mayest receive from the mouth of thine advocate, as to any fresh matters that may forward and expedite a good issue of thine affair in the court of heaven. The want of this was the reason that the deliverance of Israel did linger so long in former times. "O," says he, "that my people had hearkened unto me, *and* Israel had walked in my ways! I should soon have subdued their enemies, and turned my hand against their adversaries. The haters of the Lord should have

---

1 Micah 7:9–10.
2 Psalm 27:14.
3 Psalm 37:34.

submitted themselves unto him; but their time should have endured for ever."[1]

(e.) Also, if it tarry long, wait for it. Do not conclude that thy cause is lost because at present thou dost not hear from court. Cry, if thou wilt, O, when wilt thou come unto me? But never let such a wicked thought pass through thy heart, saying, "This evil *is* of the Lord; what should I wait for the Lord any longer?"[2]

(f.) But take heed that thou turnest not thy waiting into sleeping. Wait thou must, and wait patiently too; but yet wait with much longing and earnestness of spirit, to see or hear how matters go above. You may observe, that when a man that dwells far down in the country, and has some business at the term, in this or another of the king's courts, though he will wait his lawyer's time and conveniency, yet he will so wait as still to inquire at the post house, or at the carrier's, or if a neighbour comes down from term, at his mouth, for letters, or any other intelligence, if possibly he may arrive to know how his cause speeds, and whether his adversary, or he, has the day. Thus, I say, thou must wait upon thine Advocate. His ordinances are his post house, his ministers are his carriers, where tidings from heaven are to be had, and where those that are sued in that court by the devil may, at one time or another, hear from their lawyer, their advocate, how things are like to go. Wherefore, I say, wait at the posts of wisdom's house, go to ordinances with expectation to hear from thy Advocate there; for he will send in due time; "though it tarry, wait for it; because it will surely come, it will not tarry."[3] And now, soul, I have answered thy request, and let me hear what thou sayest unto me.

Soul.—Truly, says the soul, methinks that by what you have said, I may have this blessed Jesus to be mine Advocate; for I think, verily, I have entertained him to be mine Advocate. I have also revealed my cause unto him, yea, committed both it and myself unto him; and, as you say, I wait; oh! I wait! and my eyes fail with looking upward. Fain would I hear how my soul standeth in the sight of God, and whether my sins, which I have committed since light and grace were given unto me, be by mine Advocate, taken out of the hand of the devil, and by mine Advocate removed as far from me as the ends of the

---

[1] Psalm 81:13–15.
[2] 2 Kings 6:33.
[3] Habakkuk 2:1–3.

earth are asunder; whether the verdict has gone on my side, and what a shout there was among the angels when they saw it went well with me! But alas! I have waited, and that a long time, and have, as you advise, ran from ordinance to minister, and from minister to ordinance, or, as you phrase it, from the post to the carrier, and from the carrier to the post house, to see if I could hear aught from heaven how matters went about my soul there. I have also asked those that pass by the way, "if they saw him whom my soul loveth," and if they had anything to communicate to me? But nothing can I get or find but *generals*; as, that I have an Advocate there, and that he pleadeth the cause of his people, and that he will thoroughly plead their cause. But what he has done for ME, of that as yet I am ignorant. I doubt if my soul shall by him be effectually secured, that yet a conditional verdict will be awarded concerning me, and that much bitter will be mixed with my sweet, and that I must drink gall and wormwood for my folly; for if David, and Asa, and Hezekiah and such good men, were so served for their sins,[1] why should I look for other dealing at the hand of God? But as to this, I will endeavour to "bear the indignation of the Lord, because I have sinned against him,"[2] and shall count it an infinite mercy, if this judgment comes to me from him, that I may "not be condemned with the world."[3] I know it is dreadful walking in darkness; but if that also shall be the Lord's lot upon me; I pray God I may have faith enough to stay upon him till death, and then will the clouds blow over, and I shall see him in the light of the living.

Mine enemy, the devil, as you see, is of an inveigling temper; and though he has accused me before the judgment-seat of God, yet when he comes to me at any time, he glavers[4] and flatters as if he never did mean me harm; but I think it is that he might get further advantage against me. But I carry it now at a greater distance than formerly; and O that I was at the remotest distance, not only from him, but also from that self of mine, that laboureth with him for my undoing!

But although I say these things now, and to you, yet I have my solitary hours, and in them I have other strange thoughts;

---

1 2 Chronicles 16:7, 12.
2 Micah 7:9.
3 1 Corinthians 11:32.
4 Glaver—to wheedle, flatter, or fawn upon; now obsolete.—(OFFOR.)

for thus I think, my cause is bad, I have sinned, and I have been vile. I am ashamed myself of mine own doings, and have given mine enemy the best end of the staff. The law, and reason, and my conscience, plead for him against me, and all is true; he puts into his charge against me, that I have sinned more times than there be hairs on my head. I know not anything that ever I did in my life but it had flaw, or wrinkle, or spot, or some such thing in it. Mine eyes have seen vileness in the best of my doings; what, then, think you, must God needs see in them? Nor can I do anything yet, for all I know that I am accused by my enemy before the judgment seat of God, better than what already is imperfect. "I lie down in my shame, and my confusion covers my face." "I have sinned, what shall I do unto thee, O thou preserver of men."[1]

Reply.—Well, soul, I have heard what thou hast said, and if all be true which thou hast said, it is good, and gives me ground of hope that Jesus Christ is become thine Advocate; and if that be so, no doubt but thy trial will come to a good conclusion. And be not afraid because of the holiness of God; for thine Advocate has this for his advantage, that he pleads before a judge that is just, and against an enemy that is unholy and rejected. Nor let the thoughts of the badness of thy cause terrify thee overmuch. Cause thou hast indeed to be humble, and thou dost well to cover thy face with shame; and it is no matter how base and vile thou art in thine own eyes, provided that it comes not by renewed acts of rebellion, but through a spiritual sight of thine imperfections. Only let me advise thee here to stop. Let not thy shame nor thy self-abasing apprehension of thyself, drive thee from the firm and permanent ground of hope, which is the promise, and the doctrine of an Advocate with the Father. No; let not the apprehension of the badness of thy cause do it, forasmuch as he did never yet take cause in hand that was good, perfectly good of itself; and his excellency is, to make a man stand that has a bad cause; yea, he can make a bad cause good, in a way of justice and righteousness.

---

[1] Jeremiah 3:25; Job 7:20.

THE PRIVILEGES OF THOSE WHO HAVE CHRIST FOR AN ADVOCATE

Fourthly, And for thy further encouragement in this matter, I will here bring in the fourth chief head—to wit, *to show what excellent privilege* (I mean over and above what has already been spoken of) *they have that are made partakers of the benefit of this office:*—"If any man sin, we have an Advocate with the Father, Jesus Christ the righteous."

First Privilege. Thy Advocate pleads to a price paid, to a propitiation made; and this is a great advantage; yea, he pleads to a satisfaction made for all wrongs done, or to be done, by his elect—"For by one offering he hath perfected for ever them that are sanctified."[1] "By one offering"—that is, by the offering of himself—by one offering once offered, once offered in the end of the world. This, I say, thine Advocate pleads. When Satan brings in fresh accusations for more transgressions against the law of God, he forces not Christ to shift his first plea. I say, he puts him not to his shifts at all; for the price once paid hath in it sufficient value, would God impute it to that end, to take away the sin of the whole world. There is a man that hath brethren; he is rich, and they are poor (and this is the case betwixt Christ and us), and the rich brother goeth to his father, and saith, Thou art related to my brethren with me, and out of my store, I pray thee, let them have sufficient, and for thy satisfaction I will put into thy hand the whole of what I have, which perhaps is worth an hundred thousand pounds by the year; and this other sum I also give, that they be not disinherited. Now, will not this last his poor brethren to spend upon a great while? But Christ's worth can never be drawn dry.

1 Hebrews 10:10, 14; 9:26.

Now, set the case again, that some ill-conditioned man should take notice that these poor men live all upon the spend (and saints do so), and should come to the good man's house, and complain to him of the spending of his sons, and that while their elder brother stands by, what do you think the elder brother would reply, if he was as good-natured as Christ? Why, he would say, I have yet with my father in store for my brethren, wherefore then seekest thou to stop his hand? As he is just, he must give them for their conveniency; yea, and as for their extravagancies, I have satisfied for them so well, that, however he afflicteth them, he will not disinherit them. I hope you will read and hear this, not like them that say, "Let us do evil that good may come," but like those whom the love of Christ constrains to be better. However, this is the children's bread, that which they have need of, and without which they cannot live; and they must have it, though Satan should put pins into it, therewith to choke the dogs.[1] And for the further clearing of this, I will present you with these few considerations:

1. Those that are most sanctified have yet a body of sin and death in them, and so also it will be, while they continue in this world.[2]

2. This body of sin strives to break out, and will break out, to the polluting of the conversation, if saints be not the more watchful.[3] Yea, it has broke out in a most sad manner, and that in the strongest saints.[4]

3. Christ offereth no new sacrifice for the salvation of these his people. "For, being raised from the dead, he dieth no more."[5] So then, if saints sin, they must be saved, if saved at all, by virtue of the offering already offered; and if so, then all Christ's pleas, as an Advocate, are grounded upon that one offering which before, as a Priest, he presented God with, for the taking away of sin. So then, Christians live upon this old stock;

---

[1] This sentence at first sight seems obscure. The children's bread is the superabounding riches of Divine grace. Satan putting pins into it, may refer to those who profanely pervert the grace of God to evil, by saying, "Let us do evil, that good may come. Whose damnation is just." These are the dogs who are without, but never were within the fold of Christ. Philippians 3:2; Revelation 22:15.—(Offor.)

[2] Romans 7:24.

[3] Romans 6:12.

[4] Galatians 5:17.

[5] Romans 6:9.

their transgressions are forgiven for the sake of the worth, that yet God finds in the offering that Christ hath offered. And all Christ's pleadings, as an Advocate, are grounded upon the sufficiency and worth of that one sacrifice; I mean, all his pleadings with his Father, as to the charge which the accuser brings in against them. For though thou art a man of infirmity, and so incident to nothing [so much] as to stumble and fall, if grace doth not prevent, and it doth not always prevent; yet the value and worth of the price that was once paid for thee is not yet worn out; and Christ, as an Advocate, still pleadeth, as occasion is given, that, with success, to thy salvation. And this privilege they have, who indeed have Christ for their Advocate; and I put it here, in the first place, because all other do depend upon it.

Second Privilege. Thine Advocate, as he pleadeth a price already paid, so, and therefore, he pleads for himself as for thee. We are all concerned in one bottom; if he sinks, we sink; if we sink, he sinks.[1] Give me leave to make out my meaning.

1. Christ pleads the value and virtue of the price of his blood and sacrifice for us. And admit of this horrible supposition a little, for argument's sake, that though Christ pleads the worth of what, as Priest, he offereth, yet the soul for whom he so pleads perishes eternally. Now, where lieth the fault? In sin, you say: true; but it is because there was more virtue in sin to damn, than there was in the blood pleaded by Christ to save; for he pleaded his merit, he put it into the balance against sin; but sin hath weighed down the soul of the sinner to hell, notwithstanding the weight of merit that he did put in against it. Now, what is the result, but that the Advocate goes down, as well as we; we to hell, and he in esteem? Wherefore, I say, he is concerned with us; his credit, his honour, his glory and renown, flies all away, if those for whom he pleads as an Advocate perish for want of worth in his sacrifice pleaded. But shall this ever be said of Christ? or will it be found that any, for whom Christ as Advocate pleads, yet perish for want of worth in the price, or of neglect in the Advocate to plead it? No, no; himself is

---

[1] Dr. Watts beautifully illustrates this soul-supporting truth in his hymn (116, verse 2):—
> "How can I sink with such a prop,
>   As my eternal God,
> Who bears the earth's huge pillars up,
>   And spreads the heavens abroad?"—(OFFOR.)

concerned, and that as to his own reputation and honour, and as to the value and virtue of his blood; nor will he lose these for want of pleading for them concerned in this office.

2. I argue again; Christ, as Advocate, must needs be concerned in his plea; for that every one, for whose salvation he advocates, is his own; so, then, if he loses, he loses his own—his substance and inheritance. Thus, if he lose the whole, and if he lose a part, one, any one of his own, he loseth part of his all, and of his fulness; wherefore we may well think, that Christ, as Advocate, is concerned, even concerned with his people, and therefore will thoroughly plead their cause.

Suppose a man should have a horse, though lame, and a piece of ground, though somewhat barren, yet if any should attempt to take these away, he would not sit still, and so lose his own; no, saith he, "since they are mine own, they shall cost me five times more than they are worth, but I will maintain my right." I have seen men sometimes strongly engaged in law for that which, when considered by itself, one would think was not worth regarding; but when I have asked them, why so concerned for a thing of so little esteem? they have answered, O, it is some of that by which I hold a title of honour, or my right to a greater income, and therefore I will not lose it. Why, thus is Christ engaged; what he pleads for is his own, his all, his fulness; yea, it is that by which he holds his royalty, for he is "King of saints."[1] It is part of his estate, and that by which he holds some of his titles of honour.[2] Saviour, Redeemer, Deliverer, and Captain, are some of his titles of honour; but if he loseth any of those, upon whose account he weareth those titles of honour, for want of virtue in his plea, or for want of worth in his blood, he loseth his own, and not only so, but part of his royalty, and does also diminish and lay a blot upon his glorious titles of honour; and he is jealous of his honour; his honour he will not give to another.

Wherefore he will not, be not afraid, he never will leave nor forsake those who have given themselves unto him, and for whom he is become an Advocate with the Father, to plead their cause; even because thou art one, one of his own, one by whom he holdeth his glorious titles of honour.

Objection. O, but I am but one, and a very sorry one, too;

---

1 Revelation 15:3; John 6:37–39; Psalm 16:5–6.

2 Ephesians 5:23; Jeremiah 50:34; Romans 11:26; Hebrews 2:10.

and what is one, especially such an one as I am? Can there be a miss of the loss of such an one?

Answer. One and one makes two, and so *ad infinitum.* Christ cannot lose one, but as he may lose more, and so, in conclusion, lose all: but of all that God has given him, he will lose nothing.[1] Besides, to lose one would encourage Satan, disparage his own wisdom, make him incapable of giving in, at the day of account, the whole tale[2] to God of those that he has given him. Further, this would dishearten sinners, and make them afraid of venturing their cause and their souls in his hand; and would, as I said before, either prove his propitiation in some sense ineffectual, or else himself defective in his pleading of it; but none of these things must be supposed. He will thoroughly plead the cause of his people, execute judgment for them, bring them out to the light, and cause them to behold his righteousness.[3]

Third Privilege. The plea of Satan is groundless, and that is another privilege: for albeit thou hast sinned, yet since Christ before has paid thy debt, and also paid for more; since thou hast not yet run beyond the price of thy redemption; it must be concluded that Satan wants a good bottom to ground his plea upon, and therefore must, in conclusion, fail of his design. True, there is sin committed, there is a law transgressed, but there is also a satisfaction for this transgression, and that which superabounds; so, though there be sin, yet there wants a foundation for a plea. Joshua was clothed with filthy garments, but Christ had other garments provided for him, change of raiment; wherefore iniquity, as to the charge of Satan, vanishes. "And the angel answered and said, Take away the filthy garments from him" [this intimates that there was no ground, no sufficient ground, for Satan's charge]; "and unto him he said, Behold I have caused thine iniquity to pass from thee, and I will clothe thee with change of raiment."[4,5] Now, if there be no ground, no sound and sufficient ground, to build a charge against the child upon, I mean, as to eternal condemnation; for that is the thing contended for; then, as I said, Satan must fall

---

1 John 6:38–39.
2 The whole tale—the whole number as reckoned and ascertained; nothing being lost.—(OFFOR.)
3 Micah 7:9.
4 In the first edition of this treatise, this quotation is from Joshua 3:4, an error which has been continued through every edition to the present one.—(OFFOR.)
5 Zechariah 3:4.

"like lightning to the ground," and be cast over the bar, as a corrupt and illegal pleader. But this is so, as in part is proved already, and will be further made out by that which follows. They that have indeed Christ to be their Advocate, are themselves, by virtue of another law than that against which they have sinned, secured from the charge that Satan brings in against them. I granted before, that the child of God has sinned, and that there is a law that condemneth for this sin; but here is the thing, this child is removed by an act of grace into and under another law: "For we are not under the law," and so, consequently, "there is now no condemnation for them."[1] Wherefore, when God speaketh of his dealing with his, he saith, It shall "not be by their covenant," that is, not by that of the law, they then being not under the law.[2] What if a plea be commenced against them, a plea for sin, and they have committed sin; a plea grounded upon the law, and the law takes cognizance of their sin? Yet, I say, the plea wants a good bottom, for that the person thus accused is put under another law; hence, he says, "Sin shall not have dominion over you, for ye are not under the law." If the child was under the law, Satan's charge would be good, because it would have a substantial ground of support; but since the child is dead to the law,[3] and that also dead to him, for both are true as to condemnation,[4] how can it be that Satan should have a sufficient ground for his charge, though he should have matter of fact, sufficient matter of fact, that is sin? For by his change of relation, he is put out of the reach of that law. There is a woman, a widow, that oweth a sum of money, and she is threatened to be sued for the debt; now what doth she but marrieth; so, when the action is commenced against her as a widow, the law finds her a married woman; what now can be done? Nothing to her; she is not who she was; she is delivered from that state by her marriage; if anything be done, it must be done to her husband. But if Satan will sue Christ for my debt, he oweth *him* nothing; and as for what the law can claim of me while I was under it, Christ has delivered me by redemption from that curse, "being made a curse for me."[5]

Now the covenant into which I am brought by grace, by

---

1 Romans 6:14; 8:1.
2 Ezekiel 16:61.
3 Galatians 2:19.
4 Romans 7:6.
5 Galatians 3:13.

which also I am secured from the law, is not a law of sin and death, as that is from under which I am brought,[1] but a law of grace and life; so that Satan cannot come at me by that law; and by grace, I am by that secured also from the hand, and mouth, and sting of all other; I mean still, as to an eternal concern. Wherefore God saith, "If we break his law, the law of works, he will visit our sin with a rod, and our iniquity with stripes; but his covenant, his new covenant, will he not break," but will still keep close to that, and so secure us from eternal condemnation.[2]

Christ also is made the mediator of that covenant, and therefore an Advocate by that; for his priestly office and advocateship are included by his mediation; wherefore when Satan pleads by the old, Christ pleads by the new covenant, for the sake of which the old one is removed. "In that he saith, A new *covenant*, he hath made the first old. Now that which decayeth and waxeth old *is* ready to vanish away."[3] So, then, the ground of plea is with Jesus Christ, and not with our accuser. Now, what doth Christ plead, and what is the ground of his plea? Why, he pleads for exemption and freedom from condemnation, though by the law of works his children have deserved it; and the ground for this his plea, as to law, is the matter of the covenant itself, for thus it runs: "For I will be merciful to their unrighteousness, and their sins and their iniquities will I remember no more."[4] Now here is a foundation—a foundation in law, for our Advocate to build his plea upon; a foundation in a law not to be moved, or removed, or made to give place, as that is forced to do, upon which Satan grounds his plea against us.

Men, when they plead before a judge, use to plead matter of law. Now, suppose there is an old law in the realm, by which men deserve to be condemned to death, and there is a *new* law in this realm that secureth men from that condemnation which belongs to them by the old; and suppose also, that I am completely comprehended by all the provisoes of the new law, and not by any tittle thereof excluded from a share therein; and suppose, again, that I have a brangling adversary that pursues me by the *old* law, which yet cannot in right touch me, because

---

[1] Romans 8:2.
[2] Psalm 89:30–37.
[3] Hebrews 8:13.
[4] Hebrews 8:12.

I am interested in the new; my advocate also is one that pleads by the new law, where only there is a ground of plea; shall not now mine adversary feel the power of his plea to the delivering of me, and the putting of him to shame? Yes, verily; especially since the plea is good, the judge just; nor can the enemy find any ground for a demur[1] to be put in against my present discharge in open court, and that by proclamation; especially since my Advocate has also, by his blood, fully satisfied the old law, that he might establish the new.[2]

Fourth Privilege. Since that which goeth before is true, it follows, that he that entereth his plea against the children must needs be overthrown; for always before just judges it is the right that taketh place. Judge the right, O Lord, said David; or, "let my sentence come forth from thy presence," according to the law of grace. And he that knows what strong ground, or bottom, our Advocate has for his pleadings, and how Satan's accusations are without sound foundation, will not be afraid, he speaking in Christ, to say, I appeal to God Almighty, since Christ is my Advocate by the new law, whether I ought to be condemned to death and hell for what Satan pleads against me by the old. Satan urgeth that we have sinned, but Christ pleads to his propitiatory sacrifice; and so Satan is overthrown. Satan pleads the law of works, but Christ pleads the law of grace. Further, Satan pleads the justice and holiness of God against us; and there the accuser is overthrown again. And to them Christ appeals, and his appeal is good, since the law testifies to the sufficiency of the satisfaction that Christ has made thereto by his obedience.[3] And also, since by another covenant, God himself has given us to Jesus Christ, and so delivered us from the old. Wherefore you read nothing as an effect of Satan's pleading against us, but that his mouth is stopped, as appears by the 3rd of Zechariah; and that he is cast; yea, cast down, as you have it in the 12th of Revelations.

Indeed, when God admits not, when Christ wills not to be an Advocate, and when Satan is bid stand at the right hand of one accused, to enforce, by pleading against him, the things charged on him by the law, then he can prevail—prevail for

---

1 A demur—now called a demurrer, is when a defect or legal difficulty is discovered, which must first be settled by the judge before the action or proceedings can be carried on.—(Offor.)
2 Hebrews 10:9, 11–12.
3 Romans 3:22–23.

ever against such a wretched one.[1] But when Christ stands up to plead, when Christ espouses this or that man's cause, then Satan must retreat, then he must go down. And this necessarily flows from the text, "We have an Advocate," a prevailing one, one that never lost cause, one that always puts the children's enemy to the rout before the judgment-seat of God.[2] This, therefore, is another privilege that they have, who have Jesus Christ for their Advocate; their enemy must needs be overthrown, because both law and justice are on their side.

Fifth Privilege. Thine advocate has pity for thee, and great indignation against thine accuser; and these are two excellent things. When a lawyer hath pity for a man whose cause he pleadeth, it will engage him much; but when he has indignation also against the man's accuser, this will yet engage him more. Now, Christ has both these, and that not of humour, but by grace and justice; grace to us, and justice to our accuser. He came down from heaven that he might be a Priest, and returned thither again to be a Priest and Advocate for his; and in both these offices he levelleth his whole force and power against thine accuser: "For this purpose the Son of God was manifested, that he might destroy the works of the devil."[3]

Cunning men will, if they can, retain such an one to be their Advocate, who has a particular quarrel against their adversary; for thus, think they, he that is such, will not only plead for me, but for himself, and to right his own wrongs also; and since, if it be so, and it is so here, my concerns and my Advocate's are interwoven, I am like to fare much the better for the anger that is conceived in his heart against him. And this, I say, is the children's case; their Advocate counteth their accuser his greatest enemy, and waiteth for a time to take vengeance, and he usually then takes the opportunity when he has aught to do for his people against him. Hence he says, "The day of vengeance *is* in mine heart, and the year of my redeemed is come."[4]

I do not say that this revenge of Christ is, as ofttimes is a man's, of spite, prejudice, or other irregular lettings out of passions; but it ariseth from righteousness and truth; nor can it

---

[1] Psalm 109:6–7.
[2] How consoling a reflection is this to the distressed soul, "Christ never lost a cause." "Him that cometh to me, I will in no wise cast out." "They shall never perish; nor shall any pluck them out of my hand." John 10:28.—(Offor.)
[3] 1 John 3:8.
[4] Isaiah 63:3–4.

be but that Jesus must have a desire to take vengeance on his enemy and ours, since holiness is in him, to the utmost bounds of perfection. And I say again, that in all his pleading as an Advocate, as well as in his offering as a Priest, he has a hot and flaming desire and design to right himself upon his foe and ours; hence he triumphed over him when he died for us upon the cross, and designed the spoiling of his principality, while he poured out his blood for us before God. We then have this advantage more, in that Christ is our Advocate, our enemy is also his, and the Lord Jesus counts him so.[1]

Sixth Privilege. As thine Advocate, so thy judge holdeth thine accuser for his enemy also; for it is not of love to righteousness and justice that Satan accuseth us to God, but that he may destroy the workmanship of God. Wherefore he also fighteth against God when he accuseth the children; and this thy Father knows right well. He must therefore needs distinguish between the charge and the mind that brings it; especially when what is charged upon us is under the gracious promise of a pardon, as I have showed it is. Shall not the Judge then hear his Son—for our Advocate is his Son—in the cause of one that he favours, and that he justly can, against an enemy who seeks his dishonour, and the destruction of his eternal designs of grace?

A mention of the judge's *son* goes far with countrymen; and great striving there is with them who have great enemies and bad causes to get the judge's son to plead, promising themselves that the judge is as like to hear him, and to yield a verdict to his plea, as to any other lawyer. But what now shall we say concerning our Judge's Son, who takes part, not only with his children, but with him, and with law and justice, in pleading against our accuser? Yea, what shall we say when both Judge, and Advocate, and law, are all bent to make our persons stand and escape, whatever, and how truly soever, the charge and accusation is by which we are assaulted of the devil. And yet all this is true; wherefore, here is another privilege of them that have Jesus for their Advocate.

Seventh Privilege. Another privilege that they have who have Jesus Christ for their Advocate is, that he is undaunted, and of a good courage, as to the cause that he undertakes; for that is a requisite qualification for a lawyer, to be bold and undaunted in a man's cause. Such an one is coveted, especially by

---
1 Colossians 2:14–15.

him that knows he has a brazen-faced antagonist. Wherefore, he saith that "he will set his face like a flint," when he stands up to plead the cause of his people.[1] Lawyers, of all men, need this courage, and to be above others, men of hard foreheads, because of the affronts that sometimes they meet with, be their cause never so good, in the face sometimes, of the chief of a kingdom. Now Christ is our lawyer and stands up to plead, not only sometimes, but always, for his people, before the God of gods, and that not in a corner, but while all the host of heaven stands by, both on the right hand and on the left. Nor is it to be doubted but that our accuser brings many a sore charge against us into the court; but, however, we have an Advocate that is valiant and courageous, one that will not fail nor be discouraged till he has brought judgment unto victory. Hence John asserts his name, saying, "If any man sin, we have an Advocate with the Father, Jesus Christ."

Men love to understand a man before they commit their cause unto him—to wit, whether he be fitly qualified for their business. Well, here is an Advocate propounded, an Advocate to plead our cause against our foe. But what is he? What is his name? Is he qualified for my business? The answer is, It is Jesus Christ. How? Jesus Christ, what! that old friend of publicans and sinners? Jesus Christ! he used never to fail, he used to set his face like a flint against Satan when he pleaded the cause of his people. Is it Jesus Christ? says the knowing soul; then he shall be mine Advocate.

For my part, I have often wondered, when I have considered what sad causes Jesus Christ sometimes takes in hand, and for what sad souls he sometimes pleads with God his Father. He had need of a face as hard as flint, else how could he bear up in that work in which for us sometimes he is employed—a work enough to make angels blush. Some, indeed, will lightly put off this, and say, "It is his office;" but, I say, his office, notwithstanding the work in itself is hard, exceeding hard, when he went to die, had he not despised the shame, he had turned his back upon the cross, and left us in our blood. And now it is his turn to plead, the case would be the same, only he can make argument upon that which to us seems to yield no argument at all, to take courage to plead for a Joshua, for a Joshua clothed, clothed with filthy garments. He, saith he, that "shall

---
[1] Isaiah 50:5–7.

be ashamed of me and of my words in this adulterous and sinful generation: of him shall the Son of man be ashamed," etc.[1] Hence it follows that Christ will be ashamed of some; but why not ashamed of others? It is not because their cause is good, but because they are kept from denying of him professedly; wherefore, for such he will force himself, and will set his face like a flint, and will, without shame, own, plead, and improve his interest with God for them, even for them whose cause is so horribly bad and gross that themselves do blush while they think thereof. But what will not love do? what will not love bear with? and what will not love suffer? Of all the offices of Jesus Christ, I think this trieth him as much as any! True, his offering himself in sacrifice tried him greatly, but that was but for awhile; his grappling, as a captain, with the curse, death, and hell, tried him much, but that also was but for a while; but this office of being an Advocate, though it meeteth not with such sudden depths of trouble, yet what it wants in shortness it may meet with in length of time. I know Christ, being raised from the dead, dies no more; yet he has not left off, though in heaven, to do some works of service for his saints on earth; for there he pleads as an Advocate or lawyer for his people.[2] And let it be that he has no cause of shame when he standeth thus up to plead for so vile a wretch as I, who have so vilely sinned, yet I have cause to think that well he may, and to hold my hands before my face for shame, and to be confounded with shame, while he, to fetch me off from condemnation for my transgressions, sets his face like a flint to plead for me with God, and against my accuser. But thus much for the seventh privilege that they have by Christ who have him for their Advocate.

Eighth Privilege. Another privilege that they have who have Jesus Christ to be their Advocate is this, He is always ready, always in court, always with the judge, then and there to oppose, if our accuser comes, and to plead against him what is pleadable for his children. And this the text implies where it saith, "We have an Advocate with the Father," always with the Father. Some lawyers, though they are otherwise able and shrewd, yet not being always in court and ready, do suffer their poor clients to be baffled and nonsuited[3] by their adversary;

---
1 Mark 8:38.
2 Hebrews 8:1–2.
3 Nonsuit—the giving up a suit upon the discovery of some fatal error or defect in the cause.—(Offor.)

yea, it so comes to pass because of this neglect, that a judgment is got out against them for whom they have undertaken to plead, to their great perplexity and damage: but no such opportunity can Satan have of our Advocate, for he is with the Father, always with the Father; as to be a Priest, so to be an Advocate—"We have an Advocate with the Father." It is said of the priests, they wait at the altar, and that they give attendance there,[1] also of the magistrate, that as to his office, he should attend "continually on this very thing."[2] And as these, so Christ, as to his office of an Advocate, attends continually upon that office with his Father. "We have an Advocate with the Father," always with the Father. And truly such an Advocate becomes the children of God, because of the vigilancy of their enemy; for it is said of him, that "he accuseth us day and night," so unweariedly doth he both seek and pursue our destruction.[3] But behold how we are provided for him—"We have an Advocate with the Father." If he come a-days, our Advocate is with the Father; if he come a-nights, our Advocate is with the Father.[4] Thus, then, is our Advocate ready to put check to Satan, come he when he will or can, to accuse us to the Father. Wherefore these two texts are greatly to be minded, one of them, for that it shows us the restlessness of our enemy, the other, for that it shows us the diligence of our Advocate.

That, also, in the Hebrews shows us the carefulness of our Advocate, where it saith, He is gone "into heaven itself, now to appear in the presence of God for us."[5] Now, just the time present; NOW, the time always present; NOW, let Satan come when he will! Nor is it to be omitted that this word that thus specifies the time, the present time, doth also conclude it to be that time in which we are imperfect in grace, in which we have many failings, in which we are tempted and accused of the devil to God; this is the time, and in it, and every whit of it, he now appeareth in the presence of God for us. Oh, the diligence of our enemy; oh, the diligence of our friend!—the one against us, the other for us, and that continually—"If any man sin, we have an Advocate with the Father, Jesus Christ the righteous." This,

---

[1] 1 Corinthians 9:13.
[2] Romans 13:6.
[3] Revelation 12:10.
[4] There is no night in heaven; it is one eternal day; no need of rest or sleep. Christ *ever* liveth to make intercession for us.—(OFFOR.)
[5] Hebrews 9:24.

then, that Jesus Christ is always an Advocate with the Father for us, and so continually ready to put a check to every accusation that Satan brings into the presence of God against us, is another of the privileges that they have, who have Jesus Christ for their Advocate.

Ninth Privilege. Another privilege that they have who have Jesus Christ to be their Advocate is this, he is such an one that will not, by bribes, by flattery, nor fair pretences, be turned aside from pursuing of his client's business. This was the fault of lawyers in old time, that they would wrest judgment for a bribe. Hence the Holy One complained, that a bribe did use to blind the eyes of the wise, and pervert the judgment of the righteous.[1]

There are three things in judgment that a lawyer must take heed of—one is the nature of the offence, the other is the meaning and intendment of the law-makers, and a third is to plead for them in danger, without respect to affection or reward; and this is the excellency of our Advocate, he will not, cannot be biased to turn aside from doing judgment. And this the apostle intendeth when he calleth our Advocate "Jesus Christ the righteous." "We have an Advocate with the Father, Jesus Christ the righteous;" or, as another prophet calls him, to wit, "The just Lord—one that will not do iniquity"—that is, no unrighteousness in judgment.[2] He will not be provoked to do it, neither by the continual solicitations of thine enemy; nor by thy continual provocations wherewith, by reason of thy infirm condition, thou dost often tempt him to do it. And remember that thy Advocate pleads by the new covenant, and thine adversary accuses by the old; and again, remember that the new covenant is better and more richly provided with grounds of pleading for our pardon and salvation, than the old can be with grounds for a charge to be brought in by the devil against us, suppose our sin be never so heinous. It is a better covenant, established upon better promises.

Now, put these two together—namely, that Jesus Christ is righteous, and will not swerve in judgment; also, that he pleads for us by the new law, with which Satan hath nothing to do, nor, had he, can he by it bring in a plea against us, because that law, in the very body of it, consists in free promises

---

1 1 Samuel 12:3; Amos 5:12; Deuteronomy 16:19.
2 Zephaniah 3:5.

of giving grace unto us, and of an everlasting forgiveness of our sin.[1] O children, your Advocate will stick to the law, to the new law, to the new and everlasting covenant, and will not admit that anything should be pleaded by our foe that is inconsistent with the promise of the gift of grace, and of the remission of all sin. This, therefore, is another privilege that they are made partakers of who have Jesus Christ to be their Advocate. He is just, he is righteous, he is "Jesus Christ the righteous;" he will not be turned aside to judge awry, either of the crime or the law, for favour or affection. Nor is there any sin but what is pardonable committed by those that have chosen Jesus Christ to be their Advocate.

Tenth Privilege. Another privilege that they have who have Jesus Christ to be their Advocate, is this, the Father has made him, even him that is thine Advocate, the umpire and judge in all matters that have, do, or shall fall out betwixt him and us. Mark this well; for when the judge himself, before whom I am accused, shall make mine Advocate, the judge of the nature of the crime for which I am accused, and of matter of law by which I am accused—to wit, whether it is in force against me to condemnation, or whether by the law of grace I am set free, especially since my Advocate has espoused my cause, promised me deliverance, and pleaded my right to the state of eternal life—must it not go well with me? Yes, verily. The judge, then, making thine Advocate the judge, for he "hath committed all judgment unto the Son," hath done it also for thy sake who hast chosen him to be thine Advocate.[2] It was a great thing that happened to Israel when Joseph was become their advocate, and when Pharaoh had made him a judge. "Thou," says he, "shalt be over my house, and according unto thy word shall all my people be ruled. See, I have set thee over all the land of Egypt . . . and without thee shall no man lift up his hand or foot in all the land of Egypt . . . only in the throne will I be greater than thou."[3] Joseph in this was a type of Christ, and his government here of the government of Christ for his church. Kings seldom make a man's judge his advocate; they seldom leave the issue of the whole affair to the arbitration of the poor man's lawyer; but when they do, methinks it should even go to the heart's

---

[1] Jeremiah 31:31–34; Ezekiel 36:25–30; Hebrews 8:8–13.
[2] John 5:22.
[3] Genesis 41:40, 44.

desire of the client whose the advocate is, especially when, as I said before, the cause of the client is become the concern of the advocate, and that they are both wrapt up in the self-same interest; yea, when the judge himself also is therein concerned; and yet thus it is with that soul who has Jesus Christ for his Advocate. What sayest thou, poor heart, to this? The judge—to wit, the God of heaven, has made thy Advocate, arbitrator in thy business; he is to judge; God has referred the matter to him, and he has a concern in thy concern, an interest in thy good speed. Christian man, dost thou hear? Thou hast put thy cause into the hand of Jesus Christ, and hast chosen him to be thine Advocate to plead for thee before God and against thy adversary; and God has referred the judgment of that matter to thy Advocate, so that he has power to determine the matter. I know Satan is not pleased with this. He had rather things should have been referred to himself, and then woe had been to the child of God; but, I say, God has referred the business to Jesus Christ, has made him umpire and judge in thine affair. Art thou also willing that he should decide the matter? Canst thou say unto him as David, "Judge me, O God, and plead my cause?"[1] Oh, the care of God towards his people, and the desire of their welfare! He has provided them an Advocate, and he has referred all causes and things that may by Satan be objected and brought in against us, to the judgment and sentence of Christ our Advocate. But to come to a conclusion for this; and therefore,

Eleventh Privilege. The advantage that he has that has the Lord Jesus for his Advocate is very great. Thy Advocate has the cause, has the law, has the judge, has the purse, and so consequently has all that is requisite for an Advocate to have, since together with these he has heart, he has wisdom, he has courage, and loves to make the best improvement of his advantages for the benefit of his client; and that which adds to all is, he can prove the debt paid, about which Satan makes such ado—a price given for the ransom of my soul and for the pardon of my sins. Lawyers do use to make a great matter of it, when they can prove, that that very debt is paid for which their client is sued at law. Now this Christ Jesus himself is witness to; yea, he himself has paid it, and that out of his own purse, for us, with his own hands, before and upon the mercy-seat, according

---
1 Psalm 43:1.

as the law requireth.¹ What then can accrue to our enemy? or what advantage can he get by his thus vexing and troubling the children of the Most High? Certainly nothing, but, as has been said already, to be cast down; for the kingdom of our God, which is a kingdom of grace, and the power of his Christ will prevail. Samson's power lay in his hair, but Christ's power, his power to deliver us from the accusation and charge of Satan, lieth in the worth of his undertakings. And hence it is said again, "And they overcame him by the blood of the Lamb," and he was cast out and down.² And thus much for the privileges that those are made partakers of, who have Jesus Christ to be their Advocate.

---

1 Leviticus 16:13–15; Hebrews 9:11–24.
2 Revelation 12:10–12.

THE NECESSITY OF HAVING
CHRIST FOR OUR ADVOCATE

Fiftly, I come now to the fifth thing, which is, *to show you what necessity there is that Christ should be our Advocate.*

That Christ should be a Priest to offer sacrifice, a King to rule, and a Prophet to teach, all seeing men acknowledge is of necessity; but that he should be an Advocate, a pleader for his people, few see the reason of it. But he is an Advocate, and as an Advocate has a work and employ distinct from his priestly, kingly, or prophetical offices. John says, "He is our Advocate," and signifieth also the nature of his work as such, in that very place where he asserteth his office; as also I have showed you in that which goes before. But having already showed you the nature, I will now show you the necessity of this office.

First. It is necessary for the more full and ample vindication of the justice of God against all the cavils of the infernal spirits. Christ died on earth to declare the justice of God to men in his justifying the ungodly. God standeth upon the vindication of his justice, as well as upon the act thereof. Hence the Holy Ghost, by the prophets and apostles, so largely disputeth for the vindication thereof, while it asserteth the reality of the pardon of sin, the justification of the unworthy, and their glorification with God.[1] I say, while it disputeth the justness of this high act of God against the cavils of implacable sinners. Now the prophets and apostles, in those disputes by which they seek to vindicate the justice of God in the salvation of sinners, are not only ministers of God to us, but advocates for him; since, as Elihu has it, they "speak on God's behalf," or, as the margin has it, "I will show thee that there are yet words for God," words

---
1 Romans 3:24; Isaiah, Jeremiah, Malachi, Romans 3, 4, 8; Galatians 3, 4.

to be spoken and pleaded against his enemies for the justification of his actions.[1] Now, as it is necessary that there should be advocates for God on earth to plead for his justice and holiness, while he saveth sinners, against the cavils of an ungodly people, so it is necessary that there should be an Advocate also in heaven, that may there vindicate the same justice and holiness of God from all those charges that the fallen angels are apt to charge it with, while it consenteth that we, though ungodly, should be saved.

That the fallen angels are bold enough to charge God to his face with unjustness of language, is evident in the 1st and 2nd of Job; and that they should not be as bold to charge him with unjustness of actions, nothing can be showed to the contrary. Further, that God seeks to clear himself of this unjust charge of Satan is as manifest; for all the troubles of his servant Job were chiefly for that purpose. And why he should have one also in heaven to plead for the justness of his doing in the forgiveness and salvation of sinners appears also as necessary, even because there is one, even an Advocate with the Father, or on the Father's side, seeking to vindicate his justice, while he pleadeth with him for us, against the devil and his objections. God is wonderfully pleased with his design in saving of sinners; it pleases him at the heart. And since he also is infinitely just, there is need that an Advocate should be appointed to show how, in a way of justice as well as mercy, a sinner may be saved.

The good angels did not at first see so far into the mysteries of the gospel of the grace of God, but that they needed further light therein for the vindication of their Lord as servants. Wherefore they yet did pry and look narrowly into it further, and also bowed their heads and hearts to learn yet more, by the church, of "the manifold wisdom of God."[2] And if the standing angels were not yet, to the utmost, perfect in the knowledge of this mystery, and yet surely they must know more thereof than those that fell could do, no wonder if those devils, whose enmity could not but animate their ignorance, made, and do make, their cavils against justice, insinuating that it is not impartial and exact, because it, as it is just, justifieth the ungodly.

That Satan will quarrel with God I have showed you, and

---
1 Job 36:2.
2 1 Peter 1:12; Ephesians 3:9–10.

that he will also dispute against his works with the holy angels, is more than intimated by the apostle Jude, verse 9, and why not quarrel with, and accuse the justice of God as unrighteous, for consenting to the salvation of sinners, since his best qualifications are most profound and prodigious attempts to dethrone the Lord God of his power and glory.

Nay, all this is evident, since "we have an Advocate with the Father, Jesus Christ the righteous." And again, I say, it is evident that one part of his work as an Advocate, is to vindicate the justice of God while he pleadeth for our salvation, because he pleadeth a propitiation; for a propitiation respects God as well as us; the appeasing his wrath, and the reconciling of his justice to us, as well as the redeeming us from death and hell; yea, it therefore doth the one, because it doth the other. Now, if Christ, as an Advocate, pleadeth a propitiation with God, for whose conviction doth he plead it? Not for God's; for he has ordained it, allows it, and gloriously acquiesces therein, because he knows the whole virtue thereof. It is therefore for the conviction of the fallen angels, and for the confounding of all those cavils that can be invented and objected against our salvation by those most subtle and envious ones. But,

Second. There is matter of law to be objected, and that both against God and us; at least, there seems to be so, because of the sanction that God has put upon the law, and also because we have sinned against it.

God has said, "In the day thou eatest thereof, thou shalt surely die;" and, "the soul that sinneth, it shall die." God also standeth still upon the vindication of his justice, he also saveth sinners. Now, in comes our accuser, and chargeth us of sin, of being guilty of sin, because we have transgressed the law. God also will not be put out of his way, or steps of grace, to save us; also he will say, he is just and righteous still. Ay, but these are but say-so's. How shall this be proved? Why, now, here is room for an advocate that can plead to matter of law, that can preserve the sanction of the law in the salvation of the sinner—"He will magnify the law, and make *it* honourable."[1] The margin saith, "and make him honourable"[2]—that is, he shall save the

---

1 Isaiah 42:21.

2 The marginal readings which are found in our venerable version of the Bible are very interesting, both to the unlearned and to the scholar. They often throw a light upon the Scripture. For "and make him honourable," see Bishop Patrick and Dr. Gill's annotations.—(OFFOR.)

sinner, and preserve the holiness of the law, and the honour of his God. But who is this that can do this? "It is the servant of God," saith the prophet,[1] "the Lord, a man of war." But how can this be done by him? The answer is, It shall be done, "for God is well pleased for his righteousness' sake;" for it is by that he magnifies the law, and makes his Father honourable—that is, he, as a public person, comes into the world under the law, fulfils it, and having so done, he gives that righteousness away, for he, as to his own person, never had need thereof; I say, he gives that righteousness to those that have need, to those that have none of their own, that righteousness might be imputed to them. This righteousness, then, he presenteth to God for us, and God, for this righteousness' sake, is well pleased that we should be saved, and for it can save us, and secure his honour, and preserve the law in its sanction. And this Christ pleadeth against Satan as an Advocate with the Father for us; by which he vindicates his Father's justice, holdeth the child of God, notwithstanding his sins, in a state of justification, and utterly overthroweth and confoundeth the devil.

For Christ, in pleading thus, appeals to the law itself, if he has not done it justice, saying, "Most mighty law, what command of thine have I not fulfilled? what demand of thine have I not fully answered? where is that jot or tittle of the law that is able to object against my doings for want of satisfaction?" Here the law is mute; it speaketh not one word by way of the least complaint, but rather testifies of this righteousness that it is good and holy.[2] Now, then, since Christ did this as a public person, it follows that others must be justified thereby; for that was the end and reason of Christ's taking on him to do the righteousness of the law. Nor can the law object against the equity of this dispensation of heaven; for why might not that God, who gave the law his being and his sanction, dispose as he pleases of the righteousness which it commendeth? Besides, if men be made righteous, they are so; and if by a righteousness which the law commendeth, how can fault be found with them by the law? Nay, it is "witnessed by the law and the prophets," who consent that it should be unto all, and upon all them that believe, for their justification.[3]

---

1 Isaiah 42:1, 13.
2 Romans 3:22–23; 5:15–19.
3 Romans 3:20–21.

And that the mighty God suffereth the prince of the devils to do with the law what he can, against this most wholesome and godly doctrine; it is to show the truth, goodness, and permanency thereof; for this is as who should say, Devil, do thy worst! When the law is in the hand of an easy pleader, though the cause that he pleadeth be good, a crafty opposer may overthrow the right; but here is the salvation of the children in debate, whether it can stand with law and justice; the opposer of this is the devil, his argument against it is the law; he that defends the doctrine is Christ the Advocate, who, in his plea, must justify the justice of God, defend the holiness of the law, and save the sinner from all the arguments, pleas, stops, and demurs that Satan is able to put in against it. And this he must do fairly, righteously, simply, pleading the voice of the selfsame law for the justification of what he standeth for, which Satan pleads against it; for though it is by the new law that our salvation comes, yet by the old law is the new law approved of and the way of salvation thereby by it consented to.

This shows, therefore, that Christ is not ashamed to own the way of our justification and salvation, no, not before men and devils. It shows also that he is resolved to dispute and plead for the same, though the devil himself shall oppose it. And since our adversary pretends a plea in law against it, it is meet that there should be an open hearing before the Judge of all about it; but, forasmuch as we neither can nor dare appear to plead for ourselves, our good God has thought fit we should do it by an advocate: "We have an Advocate with the Father, Jesus Christ the righteous." This, therefore, is the second thing that shows the need that we have of an Advocate—to wit, our adversary pretends that he has a plea in law against us, and that by law we should be otherwise disposed of than to be made possessors of the heavenly kingdom. But,

Third. There are many things relating to the promise, to our life, and to the threatenings, that minister matter of question and doubt, and give the advantage of objections unto him that so eagerly desireth to be putting in cavils against our salvation, all which it hath pleased God to repel by Jesus Christ our Advocate.

1. There are many things relating to the promises, as to the largeness and straitness of words, as to the freeness and conditionality of them, which we are not able so well to understand;

and, therefore, when Satan dealeth with us about them, we quickly fall to the ground before him; we often conclude that the words of the promise are too narrow and strait to comprehend us; we also think, verily, that the conditions of some promises do utterly shut us out from hope of justification and life; but our Advocate, who is for us with the Father, he is better acquainted with, and learned in, this law than to be baffled out with a bold word or two, or with a subtle piece of hellish sophistication.[1] He knows the true purport, intent, meaning, and sense of every promise, and piece of promise that is in the whole Bible, and can tell how to plead it for advantage against our accuser, and doth so. And I gather it not only from his contest with Satan for Joshua,[2] and from his conflict with him in the wilderness,[3] and in heaven,[4] but also from the practice of Satan's emissaries here; for what his angels do, that doth he. Now there is here nothing more apparent than that the instruments of Satan do plead against the church, from the pretended intricacy, ambiguity, and difficulty of the promise; whence I gather, so doth Satan before the tribunal of God; but there we have one to match him; "we have an Advocate with the Father," that knows law and judgment better than Satan, and statute and commandment better than all his angels; and by the verdict of our Advocate, all the words, and limits, and extensions of words, with all conditions of the promises, are expounded and applied! And hence it is that it sometimes so falleth out that the very promise we have thought could not reach us, to comfort us by any means, has at another time swallowed us up with joy unspeakable. Christ, the true Prophet, has the right understanding of the Word as an Advocate, has pleaded it before God against Satan, and having overcome him at the common law, he hath sent to let us know it by his good Spirit, to our comfort, and the confusion of our enemy. Again,

2. There are many things relating to our lives that minister to our accuser occasions of many objections against our salvation; for, besides our daily infirmities, there are in our lives gross sins, many horrible backslidings; also we ofttimes suck and drink in many abominable errors and deceitful opinions, of

---

1 Isaiah 50:4.
2 Zechariah 3.
3 Matthew 4.
4 Revelation 14.

all which Satan accuseth us before the judgment seat of God, and pleadeth hard that we may be damned for ever for them. Besides, some of these things are done after light received, against present convictions and dissuasions to the contrary, against solemn engagements to amendment, when the bonds of love were upon us.[1] These are crying sins; they have a loud voice in themselves against us, and give to Satan great advantage and boldness to sue for our destruction before the bar of God; nor doth he want skill to aggravate and to comment profoundly upon all occasions and circumstances that did attend us in these our miscarriages—to wit, that we did it without a cause, also, when we had, had we had grace to have used them, many things to have helped us against such sins, and to have kept us clean and upright. "There is also a sin unto death,"[2] and he can tell how to labour, by argument and sleight of speech, to make our transgressions, not only to border upon, but to appear in the hue, shape, and figure of that, and thereto make his objection against our salvation. He often argueth thus with us, and fasteneth the weight of his reasons upon our consciences, to the almost utter destruction of us, and the bringing of us down to the gates of despair and utter destruction; the same sins, with their aggravating circumstances, as I said, he pleadeth against us at the bar of God. But there he meeteth with Jesus Christ, our Lord and Advocate, who entereth his plea against him, unravels all his reasons and arguments against us, and shows the guile and falsehood of them. He also pleadeth as to the nature of sin, as also to all those high aggravations, and proveth that neither the sin in itself, nor yet as joined with all its advantageous circumstances, can be the sin unto death,[3] because we hold the head, and have not "made shipwreck of faith,"[4] but still, as David and Solomon, we confess, and are sorry for our sins. Thus, though we seem, through our falls, to come short of the promise, with Peter,[5] and leave our transgressions as stumbling blocks to the world, with Solomon, and minister occasion of a question of our salvation among the godly, yet our Advocate fetches us off before God, and we shall be found safe and in heaven at last, by them in the next world, who were afraid they had lost us in this.

---

1 Jeremiah 2:20.
2 1 John 5:16.
3 Colossians 2:19.
4 1 Timothy 1:19.
5 Hebrews 4:1–3.

But all these points must be managed by Christ for us, against Satan, as a lawyer, an advocate, who to that end now appears in the presence of God for us, and wisely handleth the very crisis of the word, and of the failings of his people, together with all those nice and critical juggles by which our adversary laboureth to bring us down, to the confusion of his face.

3. There are also the threatenings that are annexed to the gospel, and they fall now under our consideration. They are of two sorts—such as respect those who altogether neglect and reject the gospel, or those that profess it, yet fall in or from the profession thereof.

The first sort of threatening cannot be pleaded against the professors of the gospel as against those that never professed it; wherefore he betaketh himself to manage those threatenings against us that belong to those that have professed, and that have fallen from it.[1] Joshua fell in it.[2] Judas fell from it, and the accuser stands at the right hand of them before the judgment of God, to resist them, by pleading the threatenings against them—to wit, that God's soul should have no pleasure in them. "If *any man* draw back, my soul shall have no pleasure in him." Here is a plea for Satan, both against the one and the other; they are both apostatized, both drawn back, and he is subtle enough to manage it.

Ay, but Satan, here is also matter sufficient for a plea for our Advocate against thee, forasmuch as the next words distinguish betwixt drawing back, and drawing back "unto perdition;" every one that draws back, doth not draw back unto perdition.[3] Some of them draw back from, and some in the profession of, the gospel. Judas drew back *from*, and Peter *in* the profession of his faith; wherefore Judas perishes, but Peter turns again, because Judas drew back unto perdition, but Peter yet believed to the saving of the soul.[4] Nor doth Jesus Christ, when he sees it is to no boot, at any time step in to endeavour to save the soul. Wherefore, as for Judas, for his backsliding from the faith, Christ turns him up to Satan, and leaveth him in his

---

1 Psalm 109:6.
2 Zechariah 3:1–2.
3 Hebrews 10:38–39.
4 To draw back *from*, or *in*, our dependence upon Christ for salvation, is a distinction which every despairing backslider should strive to understand. The total abandonment of Christianity is perdition, while he who is overcome of evil may yet repent to the salvation of the soul.—(Offor.)

hand, saying, "When he shall be judged, let him be condemned: and let his prayer become sin."[1] But he will not serve Peter so—"The Lord will not leave him in his hand, nor condemn him when he is judged."[2] He will pray for him before, and plead for him after, he hath been in the temptation, and so secure him, by virtue of his advocation, from the sting and lash of the threatening that is made against final apostacy. But,

Fourth. The necessity of the Advocate's office in Jesus Christ appears plainly in this—to plead about the judgments, distresses, afflictions, and troubles that we meet withal in this life for our sins. For though, by virtue of this office, Christ fully takes us off from the condemnation that the unbelievers go down to for their sins, yet he doth not thereby exempt us from temporal punishments, for we see and feel that they daily overtake us; but for the proportioning of the punishment, or affliction for transgression, seeing that comes under the sentence of the law, it is fit that we should have an Advocate that understands both law and judgment, to plead for equal distribution of chastisement, according, I say, to the law of grace; and this the Lord Jesus doth.

Suppose a man for transgression be indicted at the assizes; his adversary is full of malice, and would have him punished sorely, beyond what by the law is provided for such offence; and he pleads that the judge will so afflict and punish as he in his malicious mind desireth. But the man has an advocate there, and he enters his plea against the cruelty of his client's accuser, saying, My lord, it cannot be as our enemy would have it; the punishment for these transgressions is prescribed by that law that we here ground our plea upon; nor may it be declined to satisfy his envy; we stand here upon matters of law, and appeal to the law. And this is the work of our Advocate in heaven. Punishments for the sin of the children come not headlong, not without measure, as our accuser would have them, nor yet as they fall upon those who have none to plead their cause.[3] Hath he smote the children according to the stroke wherewith he hath smitten others? No; "in measure when it shooteth forth," or seeks to exceed due bounds, "thou wilt debate with it: he

---

1 Psalm 109:7.

2 Psalm 37:33.

3 "Like as a father pitieth his children, so the Lord pitieth them that fear him." He punishes but to restore them in his own time to the paths of peace.—(Offor.)

stayeth his rough wind in the day of the east wind."[1] "Thou wilt debate with it," inquiring and reasoning by the law, whether the shootings forth of the affliction (now going out for the offence committed) be not too strong, too heavy, too hot, and of too long a time admitted to distress and break the spirit of this Christian; and if it be, he applies himself to the rule to measure it by, he fetches forth his plumb line, and sets it in the midst of his people,[2] and lays righteousness to that, and will not suffer it to go further; but according to the quality of the transgression, and according to the terms, bounds, limits, and measures which the law of grace admits, so shall the punishment be. Satan often saith of us when we have sinned, as Abishai said of Shimei after he had cursed David, Shall not this man die for this?[3] But Jesus, our Advocate, answers as David, What have I to do with thee, O Satan? Thou this day art an enemy to me; thou seekest for a punishment for the transgressions of my people above what is allotted to them by the law of grace, under which they are, and beyond what their relation that they stand in to my Father and myself will admit. Wherefore, as Advocate, he pleadeth against Satan when he brings in against us a charge for sins committed, for the regulating of punishments, both as to the nature, degree, and continuation of punishment; and this is the reason why, when we are judged, we are not condemned, but chastened, "that we should not be condemned with the world."[4] Hence king David says, the Lord hath not given him over to the will of his enemy.[5] And again, "The Lord hath chastened me sore; but he hath not given me over unto death."[6] Satan's plea was, that the Lord would give David over to his will, and to the tyranny of death. No, says our Advocate, that must not be; to do so would be an affront to the covenant under which grace has put them; that would be to deal with them by a covenant of works, under which they are not. There is a rod for children; and stripes for those of them that transgress. This rod is in the hand of a Father, and must be used according to the law of that relation, not for the destruction, but correction of the children; not to satisfy the rage of Satan,

---

1 Isaiah 27:8.
2 Amos 7:8; Isaiah 28:7.
3 2 Samuel 19:21.
4 1 Corinthians 11:32.
5 Psalm 27:12.
6 Psalm 118:18.

but to vindicate the holiness of my Father; not to drive them further from, but to bring them nearer to their God. But,

Fifth. The necessity of the advocateship of Jesus Christ is also manifest in this, for that there is need of one to plead the efficacy of old titles to our eternal inheritance, when our interest thereunto seems questionable by reason of new transgressions. That God's people may, by their new and repeated sins, as to reason at least, endanger their interest in the eternal inheritance, is manifest by such groanings of theirs as these—"Why dost thou cast me off?"[1] "Cast me not away from thy presence."[2] And, "O God, why hast thou cast *us* off for ever?"[3] Yet I find in the book of Leviticus, that though any of the children of Israel should have sold, mortgaged, or made away with their inheritance, they did not thereby utterly make void their title to an interest therein, but it should again return to them, and they again enjoy the possession of it, in the year of jubilee. In the year of jubilee, saith God, you shall return every man to his possession; "the land shall not be sold for ever," nor be quite cut off, "for the land is mine; for *ye are* strangers and sojourners with me. And in all the land of your possession, ye shall grant a redemption for the land."[4]

The man in Israel that, by waxing poor, did sell his land in Canaan, was surely a type of the Christian who, by sin and decays in grace, has forfeited his place and inheritance in heaven; but as the ceremonial law provided that the poor man in Canaan should not, by his poverty, lose his portion in Canaan for ever, but that it should return to him in the year of jubilee; so the law of grace has provided that the children shall not, for their sin, lose their inheritance in heaven for ever, but that it shall return to them in the world to come.[5,6] All therefore that happeneth in this case is, they may live without the comfort of it here, as he that had sold his house in Canaan might live without the enjoyment of it till the jubilee. They may also seem to come short of it when they die, as he in Canaan did

---

[1] Psalm 43:2.
[2] Psalm 51:11.
[3] Psalm 74:1.
[4] Leviticus 25:23–24.
[5] 1 Corinthians 11:32.
[6] How full of sweet consolation is this spiritual exposition of the Levitical law. It was a type or shadow of good things which were to come. Bunyan possessed a heavenly store of these apt illustrations.—(OFFOR.)

that deceased before the year of jubilee; but as certainly as he that died in Canaan before the jubilee did yet receive again his inheritance by the hand of his relative survivor when the jubilee came, so certainly shall he that dieth, and that seemeth in his dying to come short of the celestial inheritance now, be yet admitted, at his rising again, to the repossession of his old inheritance at the day of judgment. But now here is room for a caviller to object, and to plead against the children, saying, They have forfeited their part of paradise by their sin; what right, then, shall they have to the kingdom of heaven? Now let the Lord stand up to plead, for he is Advocate for the children; yea, let them plead the sufficiency of their first title to the kingdom, and that it is not their doings can sell the land for ever. The reason why the children of Israel could not sell the land for ever was, because the Lord, their head, reserved to himself a right therein—"The land shall not be sold for ever, for the land is mine." Suppose two or three children have a lawful title to such an estate, but they are all profuse and prodigal, and there is a brother also that has by law a chief right to the same estate: this brother may hinder the estate from being sold for ever, because it is his inheritance, and he may, when the limited time that his brethren had sold their share therein is out, if he will, restore it to them again. And in the meantime, if any that are unjust should go about utterly and for ever to deprive his brethren, he may stand up and plead for them; That in law the land cannot be sold for ever, for that it is his as well as theirs, he being resolved not to part with his right. O my brethren! Christ will not part with his right of the inheritance unto which you are also born; your profuseness and prodigality shall not make him let go his hold that he hath for you of heaven; nor can you, according to law, sell the land for ever, since it is his, and he hath the principal and chief title thereto. This also gives him ground to stand up to plead for you against all those that would hold the kingdom from you for ever; for let Satan say what he can against you, yet Christ can say, "The land is mine," and consequently that his brethren could not sell it.

Yes, says Satan, if the inheritance be divided.

O but, says Christ, the land is undivided; no man has his part set out and turned over to himself; besides, my brethren yet are under age, and I am made their guardian; they have not power to sell the land for ever; the land is mine; also my

Father has made me feoffee in trust for my brethren, that they may have what is allotted them when they are all come to a perfect man, "unto the measure of the stature of the fulness of Christ."[1] And not before, and I will reserve it for them till then; and thus to do is the will of my Father, the law of the Judge, and also my unchangeable resolution. And what can Satan say against this plea? Can he prove that Christ has no interest in the saints' inheritance? Can he prove that we are at age, or that our several parts of the heavenly house are already delivered into our own power? And if he goes about to do this, is not the law of the land against him? Doth it not say that our Advocate is "Lord of all,"[2] that the kingdom is Christ's, that it is laid up in heaven for us,[3] yea, that the "inheritance which is incorruptible, undefiled, and that fadeth not away, is reserved in heaven for us, who are kept by the power of God, through faith unto salvation."[4] Thus therefore is our heavenly inheritance made good by our Advocate against the thwartings and branglings[5] of the devil; nor can our new sins make it invalid, but it abideth safe to us at last, notwithstanding our weaknesses; though, if we sin, we may have but little comfort of it, or but little of its present profits, while we live in this present world. A spendthrift, though he loses not his title, may yet lose the present benefit, but the principal will come again at last; for "we have an Advocate with the Father, Jesus Christ the righteous."

Sixth. The necessity of the advocateship of Jesus Christ for us further appears in this—to wit, for that our evidences, which declare that we have a right to the eternal inheritance, are often out of our own hand, yea, and also sometimes kept long from us, the which we come not at the sight or comfort of again but by our Advocate, especially when our evidences are taken from us, because of a present forfeiture of this inheritance to God by this or that most foul offence. Evidences, when they are thus taken away, as in David's case they were,[6] why then they are in our God's hand, laid up, I say, from the sight

---

1 Ephesians 4:13.
2 Acts 10:36.
3 Ephesians 5:5; Colossians 1:5.
4 1 Peter 1:4–5.
5 Brandlings—noisy quarrels or squabbles. "The payment of tithes is subject to many *brangles*."—*Swift*. It is now obsolete, and is substituted by *wranglings*.—(Offor.)
6 Psalm 51:12.

of them to whom they belong, till they even forget the contents thereof.[1,2]

Now when writings and evidences are out of the hand of the owners, and laid up in the court, where in justice they ought to be kept, they are not ordinarily got thence again but by the help of a lawyer—an Advocate. Thus it is with the children of God. We do often forfeit our interest in eternal life, but the mercy is, the forfeit falls into the hand of God, not of the law nor of Satan, wherefore he taketh away also our evidences, if not all, yet some of them, as he saith—"I have taken away my peace from this people, *even* loving-kindness and mercies."[3] This he took from David, and he entreats for the restoration of it, saying, "Restore unto me the joy of thy salvation, and uphold me *with thy* free Spirit."[4] And, "Lord, turn us again, cause thy face to shine, and we shall be saved."[5]

Satan now also hath an opportunity to plead against us, and to help forward the affliction, as his servants did of old, when God was but a little angry,[6] but Jesus Christ our Advocate is ready to appear against him, and to send us from heaven our old evidences again, or to signify to us that they are yet good and authentic, and cannot be gainsaid. "Gabriel," saith he, "make this *man* to understand the vision."[7] And again, saith he to another, "Run, speak to this young man, saying, Jerusalem shall be inhabited *as* towns without walls."[8] Jerusalem had been in captivity, had lost many evidences of God's favour and love by reason of her sin, and her enemy stepped in to augment her sin and sorrow; but there was a man [the angel of the Lord] "among the myrtle trees" that were in the bottom that did prevail with God to say, I am returned to Jerusalem with mercies; and then commands it to be proclaimed that his "cities through prosperity shall yet be spread abroad."[9] Thus, by virtue of our Advocate, we are either made to receive our old evidences for

---

1 2 Peter 1:5–9.
2 The poor backslider "is blind and cannot see afar off;" this does not affect his title, but is fatal to any present prospect of the enjoyment of his inheritance.—(OFFOR.)
3 Jeremiah 16:5.
4 1 Chronicles 17:13; Psalm 51:12.
5 Psalm 80:3, 7, 19.
6 Zechariah 1:15.
7 Daniel 8:16.
8 Zechariah 2:4.
9 Zechariah 1:11–17.

heaven again, or else are made to understand that they yet are good, and stand valid in the court of heaven; nor can they be made ineffectual, but shall abide the test at last, because our Advocate is also concerned in the inheritance of the saints in light. Christians know what it is to lose their evidences for heaven, and to receive them again, or to hear that they hold their title by them; but perhaps they know not how they come at this privilege; therefore the apostle tells them "they have an Advocate;" and that by him, as Advocate, they enjoy all these advantages is manifest, because his Advocate's office is appointed for our help when we sin—that is, commit sins that are great and heinous—"If any man sin, we have an Advocate."[1]

By him the justice of God is vindicated, the law answered, the threatenings taken off, the measure of affliction that for sin we undergo determined, our titles to eternal life preserved, and our comfort of them restored, notwithstanding the wit, and rage, and envy of hell. So, then, Christ gave himself for us as a priest, died for us as a sacrifice, but pleadeth justice and righteousness in a way of justice and righteousness; for such is his sacrifice, for our salvation from the death that is due to our foul or high transgressions—as an Advocate. Thus have I given you thus far, an account of the nature, end, and necessity of the Advocateship of Jesus Christ, and should now come to the use and application, only I must first remove an objection or two.

---

[1] Every sin, however comparatively small, drives us to the mediation of Christ, but it is under a sense of great sins that we feel how precious he is as an Advocate.—(OFFOR.)

OBJECTIONS REMOVED

SIXTHLY, I now come to answer some objections.

First Objection. But what need all these offices of Jesus Christ? or, what need you trouble us with these nice distinctions? It is enough for us to believe in Christ in the general, without considering him under this and that office.

Answer. The wisdom of God is not to be charged with needless doing when it giveth to Jesus Christ such variety of offices, and calleth him to so many sundry employments for us; they are all thought necessary by heaven, and therefore should not be counted superfluous by earth. And to put a question upon thy objection—What is a sacrifice without a priest, and what is a priest without a sacrifice? And the same I say of his Advocate's office—What is an advocate without the exercise of his office? and what need of an Advocate's office to be exercised, if Christ, as sacrifice and Priest, was thought sufficient by God? Each of these offices is sufficient for the perfecting the work for which it is designed; but they are not all designed for the self-same particular thing. Christ as sacrifice offereth not himself; it is Christ as Priest does that. Christ as Priest dieth not for our sins; it is Christ as sacrifice does so. Again, Christ as a sacrifice and a Priest limits himself to those two employs, but as an Advocate he launches out into a third. And since these are not confounded in heaven, nor by the Scriptures, they should not be confounded in our apprehension, nor accounted useless.

It is not, therefore, enough for us that we exercise our thoughts upon Christ in an indistinct and general way, but we must learn to know him in all his offices, and to know the nature of his offices also; our condition requires this, it requireth it, I say, as we are guilty of sin, as we have to do with God, and with our enemy the devil. As we are guilty of sin, so we need a sacrifice; and as we are also sinners, we need one perfect to present our sacrifice to God for us. We have need also of him as priest to present our persons and services to God. And since God is just, and upon the judgment seat, and since also we are subject to sin grievously, and again, since we have an accuser who will by law plead at this bar of God our sins against us, to the end we might be condemned, we have need of, and also "have an Advocate with the Father, Jesus Christ the righteous."

Alas! how many of God's precious people, for want of a distinct knowledge of Christ in all his offices, are at this day sadly baffled with the sophistications of the devil? To instance no more than this one thing—when they have committed some heinous sin after light received, how are they, I say, tossed and tumbled and distressed with many perplexities! They cannot come to any anchor in this their troubled sea; they go from promise to promise, from providence to providence, from this to that office of Jesus Christ, but forget that he is, or else understand not what it is for this Lord Jesus to be an Advocate for them. Hence they so oft sink under the fears that their sin is unpardonable, and that therefore their condition is desperate; whereas, if they could but consider that Christ is their Advocate, and that he is therefore made an Advocate to save them from those high transgressions that are committed by them, and that he waits upon this office continually before the judgment seat of God, they would conceive relief, and be made to hold up their head, and would more strongly twist themselves from under that guilt and burden, those ropes and cords wherewith by their folly they have so strongly bound themselves, than commonly they have done, or do.

Second Objection. But notwithstanding what you have said, this sin is a deadly stick in my way; it will not out of my mind, my cause being bad, but Christ will desert me.

Answer. It is true, sin is, and will be, a deadly stick and stop to faith, attempt to exercise it on Christ as considered under which of his offices or relations you will; and, above all, the sin of unbelief is "the sin that doth so," or most "easily beset us."[1] And no marvel, for it never acteth alone, but is backed, not only with guilt and ignorance, but also with carnal sense and reason. He that is ignorant of this knows but little of himself,

---

1 Hebrews 12:1–2.

or what believing is. He that undertakes to believe, sets upon the hardest task that ever was proposed to man; not because the things imposed upon us are unreasonable or unaccountable, but because the heart of man, the more true anything is, the more it sticks and stumbles thereat; and, says Christ, "Because I tell *you* the truth, ye believe me not."[1] Hence believing is called labouring,[2] and it is the sorest labour, at times that any man can take in hand, because assaulted with the greatest oppositions; but believe thou must, be the labour never so hard, and that not only in Christ in a general way, but in him as to his several offices, and to this of his being an Advocate in particular, else some sins and some temptations will not, in their guilt or vexatious trouble, easily depart from thy conscience; no, not by promise, nor by thy attempts to apply the same by faith. And this the text insinuateth by its setting forth of Christ as Advocate, as the only or best and most speedy way of relief to the soul in certain cases.

There is, then, an order that thou must observe in exercising of thy soul in a way of believing.

1. Thou must believe unto justification in general; and for this thou must direct thy soul to the Lord Christ as he is a sacrifice for sin; and as a Priest offering that sacrifice, so as a sacrifice thou shalt see him appeasing Divine displeasure for thy sin, and as a Priest spreading the skirt of his garment over thee, for the covering of thy nakedness; thus being clothed, thou shalt not be found naked.

2. This, when thou hast done as well as thou canst, thou must, in the next place, keep thine eye upon the Lord Christ as improving, as Priest in heaven, the sacrifice which he offered on earth for the continuing thee in a state of justification in thy lifetime, notwithstanding those common infirmities that attend thee, and to which thou art incident in all thy holy services or best performances.[3] For therefore is he a Priest in heaven, and by his sacrifices interceding for thee.

3. But if thy foot slippeth, if it slippeth greatly, then know thou it will not be long before a bill be in heaven preferred against thee by the accuser of the brethren; wherefore then thou must have recourse to Christ as Advocate, to plead before God thy judge against the devil thine adversary for thee.

---

1 John 8:45.
2 Hebrews 4:11.
3 Romans 5:10; Exodus 28:31–38.

4. And as to the badness of thy cause, let nothing move thee, save to humility and self-abasement, for Christ is glorified by being concerned for thee; yea, the angels will shout aloud to see him bring thee off. For what greater glory can we conceive Christ to obtain as Advocate, than to bring off his people when they have sinned, notwithstanding Satan so charging of them for it as he doth?

He gloried when he was going to the cross to die; he went up with a shout and the sound of a trumpet, to make intercession for us; and shall we think that by his being an Advocate he receives no additional glory? It is glory to him, doubtless, to bear the title of an Advocate, and much more to plead and prosper for us against our adversary, as he doth.

5. And, I say again, for thee to think that Christ will reject thee for that thy cause is bad, is a kind of thinking blasphemy against this his office and his Word; for what doth such a man but side with Satan, while Christ is pleading against him? I say, it is as the devil would have it, for it puts strength into his plea against us, by increasing our sin and wickedness. But shall Christ take our cause in hand, and shall we doubt of good success? This is to count Satan stronger than Christ; and that he can longer abide to oppose, than Christ can to plead for us. Wherefore, away with it, not only as to the notion, but also as to the heart and root thereof. Oh! when shall Jesus Christ our Lord be honoured by us as he ought? This dastardly heart of ours, when shall it be more subdued and trodden under foot of faith? When shall Christ ride Lord, and King, and Advocate, upon the faith of his people, as he should? He is exalted before God, before angels, and above all the power of the enemy; there is nothing comes behind but the faith of his people.

Third Objection. But since you follow the metaphor so close, I will suppose, if an advocate be entertained, some recompence must be given him. His fee—who shall pay him his fee? I have nothing. Could I do anything to make this advocate part of amends, I could think I might have benefit from him; but I have nothing. What say you to this?[1]

---

[1] What can we render to the Lord? is an inquiry perpetually fostered by the pride that clings to every believer. The world, and all things in it, are his already. We must, as poor trembling beggars, "take the cup of salvation and call upon the name of the Lord,"—rely upon his free gift of a full salvation. All must be done for us gratis, or we must perish. Yes, proud sinner, you must sue as a pauper, or you can never succeed.—(OFFOR.)

Answer. Similitudes must not be strained too far; but yet I have an answer for this objection. There is, in some cases, law for them that have no money; ay, law and lawyers too; and this is called a suing *in forma pauperis*;[1] and such lawyers are appointed by authority for that purpose. Indeed, I know not that it is thus in every nation, but it is sometimes so with us in England; and this is the way altogether in the kingdom of heaven before the bar of God. All is done there for us *in forma pauperis*,[1] on free cost; for our Advocate or lawyer is thereto designed and appointed of his Father.

Hence Christ is said to plead the cause, not of the rich and wealthy, but of the poor and needy; not of those that have many friends, but of the fatherless and widow; not of them that are fat and strong, but of those under sore afflictions.[2] "He shall stand at the right hand of the poor, to save *him* from those that condemn his soul," or, as it is in the margin, "from the judges of his soul."[3] This, then, is the manner of Jesus Christ with men; he doth freely what he doth, not for price nor reward, "I have raised him up," says God, "and I will direct all his ways; he shall build my city, and he shall let go my captives, not for a price nor reward."[4] <small>Spoke of Cyrus, a type of Christ.</small>

This, I say, is the manner of Jesus Christ with men; he pleads, he sues *in forma pauperis*,[1] gratis, and of mere compassion; and hence it is that you have his clients give him thanks; for that is all the poor can give. "I will greatly praise the Lord with my mouth; yea, I will praise him among the multitude. For he shall stand at the right hand of the poor, to save him from those that condemn his soul."[5]

They know but little that talk of giving to Christ, except they mean they would give him blessing and praise. He bids us come freely, take freely, and tells us that he will give and do freely.[6] Let him have that which is his own—to wit, thyself; for thou art the price of his blood. David speaks very strangely of giving to God for mercy bestowed on him; I call it strangely, because indeed it is so to reason. "What," says he, "shall I render

---

1 In the form of a pauper, one who has nothing to pay with, but is living upon alms.—(Offor.)
2 Proverbs 22:22–23; 23:10–11; 31:9.
3 Psalm 109:31.
4 Isaiah 45:13.
5 Psalm 109:30–31.
6 Revelation 22:17; 21:6.

to the Lord for all his benefits? I will take the cup of salvation, and call upon the name of the Lord" for more.[1] God has no need of thy gift, nor Christ of thy bribe, to plead thy cause; take thankfully what is offered, and call for more; that is the best giving to God. God is rich enough; talk not then of giving, but of receiving, for thou art poor. Be not too high, nor think thyself too good to live by the alms of heaven; and since the Lord Jesus is willing to serve thee freely, and to maintain thy right to heaven against thy foe, to the saving of thy soul, without price or reward, "let the peace of God rule in your hearts, to the which also ye are called," as is the rest of "the body, and be ye thankful."[2] This, then, is the privilege of a Christian—"We have an Advocate with the Father, Jesus Christ the righteous;" one that pleadeth the cause of his people against those that rise up against them, of his love, pity, and mere good-will. Lord, open the eyes of dark readers, of disconsolate saints, that they may see who is for them, and on what terms!

Fourth Objection. But if Christ doth once begin to plead for me, and shall become mine Advocate, he will always be troubled with me, unless I should, of myself, forsake him; for I am ever in broils and suits of law, action after action is laid upon me, and I am sometimes ten times in a day summoned to answer my doings before God.

Answer. Christ is not an Advocate to plead a cause or two; nor to deliver the godly from an accusation or two. "He delivereth Israel out of all his troubles,"[3] and chooses to be an Advocate for such; therefore, the godly of old did use to make, from the greatness of their troubles, and the abundance of their troublers, an argument to the Lord Christ to send and lend them help—"Have mercy upon me," saith David; "consider my trouble *which I suffer* of them that hate me."[4] And again, "Many *are* they that rise up against me; many *there be* which say of my soul, *There is* no help for him in God."[5] Yea the troubles of this man were so many and great, that his enemies began to triumph over him, saying, "*There is* no help for him in God." But could he not deliver him, or did the Lord forsake him? No, no; "Thou hast smitten," saith he, "all mine

---

1 Psalm 116:12–13.
2 Colossians 3:15.
3 Psalm 25:22; 2 Samuel 22:28.
4 Psalm 9:13.
5 Psalm 3:1–2.

enemies *upon* the cheek bone; thou hast broken the teeth of the ungodly." And as he delivereth them from their troublers, so also he pleadeth all their causes; "O Lord," saith the church, "thou hast pleaded the causes of my soul; thou hast redeemed my life."[1] Mark, troubled Christian, thou sayest thou hast been arrested ofttimes in a day, and as often summoned to appear at God's bar, there to answer to what shall be laid to thy charge. And here, for thy encouragement, thou readest that the church hath an Advocate that pleadeth the causes of her soul; that is, all her causes, to deliver her. He knows that, so long as we are in this world, we are subject to temptation and weakness, and through them made guilty of many bad things; wherefore, he hath prepared himself to our service, and to abide with the Father, an Advocate for us. As Solomon saith of a man of great wrath, so it may be said of a man of great weakness, and the best of saints are such—he must be delivered again and again,[2] yea, "many a time," saith David, "did he deliver them,"[3] to wit, more than once or twice; and he will do so for thee, if thou entertain him to be thine Advocate. Thou talkest of leaving him, but then whither wilt thou go? all else are vain things, things that cannot profit; and he will not forsake his people,[4] "though their land be filled with sin against the Holy One of Israel."[5] I know the modest saint is apt to be abashed to think what a troublesome one he is, and what a make-work he has been in God's house all his days; and let him be filled with holy blushing; but let him not forsake his Advocate.

---

1 Lamentations 3:58.
2 Proverbs 19:19.
3 Psalm 106:43.
4 1 Samuel 12:20–23.
5 Jeremiah 51:5.

THE USE AND APPLICATION

SEVENTHLY, Having thus spoken to these objections, *let us now come to make some use of the whole.* And,

Use First. I would exhort the children to consider the dignity that God hath put upon Jesus Christ their Saviour; for by how much God hath called his Son to offices and places of trust, by so much he hath heaped dignities upon him. It is said of Mordecai, that he was next to the king Ahasuerus. And what then? Why, then the greatness of Mordecai, and his high advance, must be written in the book of the Chronicles of the kings of Media and Persia, to the end his fame might not be buried nor forgotten, but remembered and talked of in generations to come.[1] Why, my brethren, God exalted Jesus of Nazareth, hath made him the only great one, having given him a name above every name—a name, did I say?—a name and glory beyond all names, and above all names, as doth witness both his being set above all, and the many offices which he executeth for God on behalf of his people. It is counted no little addition to honour when men are not only made near to the king, but also intrusted with most, if not almost with all the most weighty affairs of the kingdom. Why, this is the dignity of Christ; he is, it is true, the natural Son of God, and so high, and one that abounds with honour. But this is not all; God has conferred upon him, as man, all the most mighty honours of heaven; he hath made him Lord Mediator betwixt him and the world. This in general. And particularly, he hath called him to be his High Priest for ever, and hath sworn he shall not be changed for another.[2] He hath accepted of his offering once for ever, counting that there

---

1 Esther 10.
2 Hebrews 7:21–24.

is wholly enough in what he did once "to perfect for ever them that are sanctified;" to wit, set apart to glory.[1]

He is Captain-general of all the forces that God hath in heaven and earth, the King and Commander of his people.[2] He is Lord of all, and made "head over all *things* to the church," and is our Advocate with the Father.[3] O, the exaltation of Jesus Christ! Let Christians, therefore, in the first place, consider this. Nor can it be but profitable to them, if withal they consider that all this trust and honour is put and conferred upon him in relation to the advantage and advancement of Christians. If Christians do but consider the nearness that is betwixt Christ and them, and, withal, consider how he is exalted, it must needs be matter of comfort to them. He is my flesh and my bone that is exalted; he is my friend and brother that is thus set up and preferred. It was something to the Jews when Mordecai was exalted to honour; they had, thereby, ground to rejoice and be glad, for that one of themselves was made lord-chief by the king, and the great governor of the land, for the good of his kindred. True, when a man thinks of Christ as severed from him, he sees but little to his comfort in Christ's exaltation; but when he looks upon Christ, and can say, My Saviour, my Priest, or the chief Bishop of my soul, then he will see much in his being thus promoted to honour. Consider, then, of the glories to which God has exalted our Saviour, in that he hath made him so high. It is comely, also, when thou speakest of him, that thou name his name with some additional title, thereby to call thy mind to the remembrance, and so to the greater reverence of the person of thy Jesus; as, our Lord Jesus, our Lord and Saviour Jesus Christ, "the Apostle and High Priest of our profession, Christ Jesus."[4] Men write themselves by their titles; as, John, earl of such a place, Anthony, earl of such a place, Thomas, lord, etc. It is common, also, to call men in great places by their titles rather than by their names; yea, it also pleaseth such great ones well; as, My lord high chancellor of England, My lord privy seal, My lord high admiral, etc. And thus should Christians make mention of Jesus Christ our Lord, adding to his name some of his titles of honour; especially since

---

1 Hebrews 10:11–14.
2 Hebrews 9:25, 28.
3 Ephesians 1:22.
4 2 Peter 2:20; Hebrews 3:1, etc.

all places of trust and titles of honour conferred on him are of special favour to us. I did use to be much taken with one sect of Christians; for that it was usually their way, when they made mention of the name of Jesus, to call him "The blessed King of Glory." Christians should do thus; it would do them good; for why doth the Holy Ghost, think you, give him all these titles but that we should call him by them, and so make mention of him one to another; for the very calling of him by this or that title, or name, belonging to this or that office of his, giveth us occasion, not only to think of him as exercising that office, but to inquire, by the Word, by meditation, and one of another, what there is in that office, and what, by his exercising of that, the Lord Jesus profiteth his church.

How will men stand for that honour that, by superiors, is given to them, expecting and using all things; to wit, actions and carriages, so as that thereby their grandeur may be maintained; and saith Christ, "Ye call me Master and Lord: and ye say well; for *so* I am."[1] Christ Jesus our Lord would have us exercise ourselves in the knowledge of his glorious offices and relative titles, because of the advantage that we get by the knowledge of them, and the reverence of, and love to, him that they beget in our hearts. "That disciple," saith the text, "whom Jesus loved saith unto Peter, It is the Lord. Now when Simon Peter heard that it was the Lord, he girt *his* fisher's coat *unto him* (for he was naked), and did cast himself into the sea. And the other disciples came in a little ship:" to wit, to shore, to wait upon their Lord.[2] The very naming of him under the title of Lord, bowed their hearts forthwith to come with joint readiness to wait upon him. Let this also learn us to distinguish Christ's offices and titles, not to confound them, for he exerciseth those offices, and beareth those titles, for great reason, and to our commodity.

Every circumstance relating both to Christ's humiliation and exaltation ought to be duly weighed by us, because of that mystery of God, and of man's redemption that is wrapped therein; for as there was not a pin, nor a loop, nor a tack in the tabernacle but had in it use of instruction to the children of Israel, so there is not any part, whether more near or more remote to Christ's suffering and exaltation, but is, could we get into it, full of spiritual advantage to us.

---

1 John 13:13.
2 John 21.

To instance the water that came out of Christ's side, a thing little taken notice of either by preachers or hearers, and yet John makes it one of the witnesses of the truth of our redemption, and a confirmation of the certainty of that record that God, to the world, hath given of the sufficiency that is in his Son to save.[1]

When I have considered that the very timing of Scripture expressions, and the season of administering ordinances, have been argumentative to the promoting of the faith and way of justification by Christ, it has made me think that both myself and most of the people of God look over the Scriptures too slightly, and take too little notice of that or of those many honours that God, for our good, has conferred upon Christ. Shall he be called a King, a Priest, a Prophet, a Sacrifice, an Altar, a Captain, a Head, a Husband, a Father, a Fountain, a Door, a Rock, a Lion, a Saviour, etc., and shall we not consider these things? And shall God to all these add, moreover, that he is an Advocate, and shall we take no notice thereof, or jumble things so together, that we lose some of his titles and offices; or so be concerned with one as not to think we have need of the benefit of the rest? Let us be ashamed thus to do or think, and let us give to him that is thus exalted the glory due unto his name.

Use Second. As we should consider the titles and offices of Christ in general, so we should consider this of his being an Advocate in particular; for this is one of the reasons which induced the apostle to present him here under that very notion to us—namely, that we should have faith about it, and consider of it to our comfort—"If any man sin, we have an Advocate with the Father, Jesus Christ the righteous." "An advocate"—an advocate, as I said, is one that hath power to plead for another in this, or that, or any court of judicature. Be much therefore in the meditation of Christ, as executing of this his office for thee, for many advantages will come to thee thereby. As,

1. This will give thee to see that thou art not forsaken when thou hast sinned; and this has not in it a little relief only, but yieldeth consolation in time of need. There is nothing that we are more prone unto than to think we are forsaken when we have sinned, when for this very thing—to wit, to keep us from thinking so, is the Lord Jesus become our Advocate—"If any man sin, we have an Advocate." Christian, thou that hast

---
1 John 19:34; 1 John 3:5–9; Romans 4:9–12.

sinned, and that with the guilt of thy sin art driven to the brink of hell, I bring thee news from God—thou shalt not die, but live, for thou hast "an Advocate with the Father." Let this therefore be considered by thee, because it yieldeth this fruit.

2. The study of this truth will give thee ground to take courage to contend with the devil concerning the largeness of grace by faith, since thy Advocate is contending for thee against him at the bar of God. It is a great encouragement for a man to hold up his head in the country, when he knows he has a special friend at court. Why, our Advocate is a friend at court, a friend there ready to give the onset to Satan, come he when he will. "We have an Advocate with the Father;" an Advocate, or one to plead against Satan for us.

3. This consideration will yield relief, when, by Satan's abuse of some other of the offices of Christ, thy faith is discouraged and made afraid. Christ as a prophet pronounces many a dreadful sentence against sin; and Christ as a king is of power to execute them; and Satan as an enemy has subtilty enough to abuse both these, to the almost utter overthrow of the faith of the children of God. But what will he do with him as he is an Advocate? Will he urge that he will plead against us? He cannot; he has no such office. "Will he plead against me with his great power? no, but he would put strength into me."[1] Wherefore Satan doth all he may to keep thee ignorant of this office; for he knows that as Advocate, when he is so apprehended, the saints are greatly relieved by him, even by a believing thought of that office.

4. This consideration, or the consideration of Christ as exercising of this office, will help thee to put by that vizor wherewith Christ by Satan is misrepresented to thee, to the weakening and affrighting of thee. There is nothing more common among saints than thus to be wronged by Satan; for as he will labour to fetch fire out of the offices of Christ to burn us, so to present him to us with so dreadful and so ireful a countenance, that a man in temptation, and under guilt, shall hardly be able to lift up his face to God. But now, to think really that he is my Advocate, this heals all! Put a vizor upon the face of a father, and it may perhaps for a while fright the child; but let the father speak, let him speak in his own fatherly dialect to the child, and the vizor is gone, if not from the father's face,

---

[1] Job 23:6.

yet from the child's mind; yea, the child, notwithstanding that vizor, will adventure to creep into its father's bosom. Why, thus it is with the saints when Satan deludes and abuses them by disfiguring the countenance of Christ to their view. Let them but hear their Lord speak in his own natural dialect (and then he doth so indeed when we hear him speak as an Advocate), and their minds are calmed, their thoughts settled, their guilt made to vanish, and their faith to revive.

Indeed, the advocateship of Jesus Christ is not much mentioned in the Word, and because it is no oftener made mention of, therefore perhaps it is that some Christians do so lightly pass it over; when, on the contrary, the rarity of the thing should make it the more admirable; and perhaps it is therefore so little made mention of in the Bible, because it should not by the common sort be abused, but is as it were privately dropped in a corner, to be found by them that are for finding relief for their soul by a diligent search of the Scriptures; for Christ in this office of advocateship is only designed for the child of God, the world hath nothing therewith to do.[1] Methinks that which alone is proper to saints, and that which by God is peculiarly designed for them, they should be mightily taken withal; the peculiar treasure of kings, the peculiar privilege of saints, oh, this should be affecting to us!—why, Christ, as an Advocate, is such. "Remember me, O Lord," said the Psalmist, "with the favour *that thou bearest unto* thy people: O visit me with thy salvation; that I may see the good of thy chosen, that I may rejoice in the gladness of thy nation, that I may glory with thine inheritance."[2] The Psalmist, you see here, is crying out for a share in, and the knowledge of, the peculiar treasure of saints; and this of Christ as Advocate is such; wherefore study it, and prize it so much the more, this Advocate is ours.

(1.) Study it with reference to its peculiarity. It is for the children, and nobody else; for the children, little and great. This is children's bread; this is a mess for Benjamin; this is to be eaten in the holy place. Children use to make much of that

---

1 This Greek word is only once translated "advocate" in the New Testament; but it is used in the Gospel by John (14, 15, 16.), and translated Comforter, and applied to the Holy Spirit. Thus, the Holy Ghost is to the Christian the παράκλητος, a monitor or comforter; and our ascended Lord is the παράκλητος, or advocate before his Father's throne. Both are our counsel—the Spirit to guide, the Saviour to defend, the saints.—(Offor.)

2 Psalm 106:4–5.

which, by way of speciality, is by their relations bestowed on them—"And Naboth said to Ahab, The Lord forbid it me, that I should give the inheritance of my fathers to thee."[1] No, truly will I not. Why so? Because it was my father's gift, not in common to all, but to me in special.

(2.) Study this office in the nature of it; for therein lies the excellency of anything, even in the nature of it. Wrong thoughts of this or that abuses it, and takes its natural glory from it. Take heed, therefore, of misapprehending, while thou art seeking to apprehend Christ as thy Advocate. Men judge of Christ's offices while they are at too great a distance from them; but "let them come near," says God, "then let them speak,"[2] or as Elihu said to his friends, when he had seen them judge amiss, "Let us choose to us judgment, let us know among ourselves what *is* good."[3] So say I; study to know, rightly to know, the Advocate-office of Jesus Christ. It is one of the easiest things in the world to miss of the nature, while we speak of the name and offices of Jesus Christ; wherefore look to it, that thou study the nature of the office of his advocateship, of his advocateship for, for so you ought to consider it. There is an Advocate for, not against, the children of God—"Jesus Christ the righteous."

(3.) Study this office with reference to its efficacy and prevalency. Job says, "After my words, they spake not again."[4] And when Christ stands up to plead, all must keep silence before him. True, Satan had the first word, but Christ the last, in the business of Joshua, and such a last as brought the poor man off well, though "clothed with filthy garments."[5] Satan must be speechless after a plea of our Advocate, how rampant soever he is afore; or as Elihu has it, "They were amazed; they answered no more; they left off speaking." Shall he that speaks in righteousness give place, and he who has nothing but envy and deceit be admitted to stand his ground? Behold, the angels cover their faces when they speak of his glory, how then shall not Satan bend before him? In the days of his humiliation, he made him cringe and creep, how much more, then, now he is exalted to glory, to glory to be an Advocate, an Advocate for his people! "If any man sin, we have an Advocate with the Father, Jesus Christ the righteous."

---

1 1 Kings 21:3.
2 Isaiah 41:1.
3 Job 34:4.
4 Job 29:22.
5 Zechariah 3.

(4.) Study the faithfulness of Christ in his execution of this office, for he will not fail nor forsake them that have entertained him for their Advocate: "He will thoroughly plead their cause."[1] Faithful and true, is one of his titles; and you shall be faithfully served by him; you may boldly commit your cause unto him, nor shall the badness of it make him fail, or discourage him in his work; for it is not the badness of a cause that can hinder him from prevailing, because he hath wherewith to answer for all thy sins, and a new law to plead by, through which he will make thee a conqueror. He is also for sticking to a man to the end, if he once engages for him,[2] He will threaten and love, he will chastise and love, he will kill and love, and thou shalt find it so. And he will make this appear at the last; and Satan knows it is so now, for he finds the power of his repulses while he pleadeth for him at the bar against him. And all this is in very faithfulness.

(5.) Study also the need that thou hast of a share in the execution of the advocateship of Jesus Christ. Christians find that they have need of washing in the blood of Christ, and that they have need of being clothed with the righteousness of Christ; they also find that they have need that Christ should make intercession for them, and that by him, of necessity, they must approach God, and present their prayers and services to him; but they do not so well see that they need that Christ should also be their Advocate. And the reason thereof is this: they forget that their adversary makes it his business to accuse them before the throne of God; they consider not the long scrolls and many crimes wherewith he chargeth them in the presence of the angels of God. I say, this is the cause that the advocateship of Christ is so little considered in the churches; yea, many that have been relieved by that office of his, have not understood what he has thereby done for them.

But perhaps this is to be kept from many till they come to behold his face, and till all things shall be revealed, that Christ might have glory given him in the next world for doing of that for them which they so little thought of in this. But do not thou be content with this ignorance, because the knowledge of his advocating it for thee will yield thee present relief. Study, therefore, thine own weakness, the holiness of the judge, the

---

1 Jeremiah 50:34.
2 John 13:1–2.

badness of thy cause, the subtilty, malice, and rage, of thine enemy; and be assured that whenever thou sinnest, by and by thou art for it accused before God at his judgment seat. These things will, as it were, by way of necessity, instil into thy heart the need that thou hast of an advocate, and will make thee look as to the blood and righteousness of Jesus Christ to justify thee, so to Christ as an Advocate to plead thy cause, as did holy Job in his distresses.[1]

Use Third. Is Christ Jesus not only a priest of, and a King over, but an Advocate for his people? Let this make us stand and wonder, and be amazed at his humiliation and condescension. We read of his humiliation on earth when he put himself into our flesh, took upon him our sins, and made them as his own unto condemnation and death. And to be an advocate is an office reproachful to the malicious, if any man be such an one, for those that are base and unworthy. Yea, and the higher and more honourable the person is that pleads for such, the more he humbles himself. The word doth often in effect account him now in heaven as a servant for us, and acts of service are acts of condescension; and I am sure some acts of service have more of that in them than some; and I think when all things are considered, that Christ neither doth nor can do anything for us there, of a more condescending nature, than to become our Advocate. True, he glories in it; but that doth not show that the work is excellent in itself. It is also one of his titles of honour; but that is to show how highly God esteems of, and dignifies all his acts; and though this shall tend at last to the greatening of his honour and glory in his kingdom, yet the work itself is amazingly mean.

I speak after the manner of men. It is accounted so in this world. How ignoble and unrespectful doth a man make himself, especially to his enemy, when he undertakes to plead a bad cause, if it happeneth to be the cause of the base and unworthy! And I am sure we are, every one, so in ourselves, for whom he is become an Advocate with the Father. True, we are made worthy in him, but that is no thanks to us; as to ourselves and our cause, both are bad enough. And let us now leave off disputing, and stand amazed at his condescension; "Who *humbleth* himself to behold *the things that are* in heaven."[2] And

---

1 Job 16:21.
2 Psalm 113:6.

men of old did use to wonder to think that God should so much stoop, as to open his eyes to look upon man, or once so much as to mind him.[1] And if these be acts that speak a condescension, what will you count of Christ's standing up as an Advocate to plead the cause of his people? Must not that be much more so accounted? O, the condescension of Christ in heaven! While cavillers quarrel at such kind of language, let the saints stay themselves and wonder at it, and be so much the more affected with his grace. The persons are base, the crimes are base, with which the persons are charged; wherefore one would think that has but the reason to think, that it is a great condescension of Christ, now in heaven, to take upon him to be an Advocate for such a people, especially if you consider the openness of this work of Christ; for this thing is not done in a corner. This is done in open court.

1. With a holy and just God; for he is the judge of all, and his eyes are purer than to behold iniquity; yea, his very essence and presence is a consuming fire; yet, before and with this God, and that for such a people, Jesus Christ, the King, will be an Advocate. For one mean man to be an Advocate for the base, with one that is not considerable, is not so much; but for Christ to be an Advocate for the base, and for the base, too, under the basest consideration, this is to be wondered at. When Bathsheba, the queen, became an advocate for Adonijah unto king Solomon, you see how he flounced at her, for that his cause was bad. "And why," saith he, "dost thou ask Abishag for Adonijah? ask for him the kingdom also."[2] I told you before, that to be an advocate did run one upon hazards of reproach; and it may easily be thought that the queen did blush, when, from the king, her son, she received such a repulse; nor do we hear any more of her being an advocate; I believe she had enough of this. But oh! this Christ of God, who himself is greater than Solomon, he is become an Advocate, "an Advocate with the Father," who is the eternally just, and holy, and righteous God; and that for a people, with respect to him, far worse than could be Adonijah in the eyes of his brother Solomon. Majesty and justice are dreadful in themselves, and much more so when approached by any, especially when the cause, as to matter of fact, is bad, that the man is guilty of who is concerned in

---

1 Job 7:17; 14:1–3; Psalm 8:4; 144:3–4.
2 1 Kings 2:16–23.

the advocateship of his friend; and yet Jesus Christ is still an Advocate for us, "an Advocate with the Father."

2. Consider, also, before whom Jesus Christ doth plead as an Advocate, and that is before, or in the presence and observation of, all the heavenly host; for whilst Christ pleadeth with God for his people, all the host of heaven stand by on the right hand and on the left.[1] And though as yet there may seem to be but little in this consideration, yet Christ would have us know, and account it an infinite kindness of his to us that he will confess, and not be ashamed of us before the angels of his Father.[2] Angels are holy and glorious creatures, and, in some respect, may have a greater knowledge of the nature and baseness of sin than we while here are capable of; and so may be made to stand and wonder while the Advocate pleads with God for a people, from head to foot, clothed therewith. But Christ will not be ashamed to stand up for us before them, though they know how bad we are, and what vile things we have done. Let this, therefore, make us wonder.

3. Add to these, how unconcerned ofttimes those are with themselves, and their own desolate condition, for whom Christ, as an Advocate, laboureth in heaven with God. Alas! the soul is as far off of knowing what the devil is doing against it at God's bar as David was when Saul was threatening to have his blood, while he was hid in the field.[3] But, O true Jonathan! how didst thou plead for David! Only here thou hadst the advantage of our Advocate, thou hadst a good cause to plead; for when Saul, thy father, said, "David shall surely die," thy reply was, "Wherefore shall he be slain? What [evil] hath he done?" But Christ cannot say thus when he pleadeth for us at God's bar; nor is our present senselessness and unconcernedness about his pleading but an aggravation to our sin. Perhaps David was praying while Jonathan was playing the advocate for him before the king his father; but perhaps the saint is sleeping, yea, sinning more, whilst Christ is pleading for him in heaven. Oh! this should greatly affect us; this should make us wonder; this should be so considered by us, as to heighten our souls to admiration of the grace and kindness of Christ.

4. Join to these the greatness and gravity, the highness

---

[1] Matthew 10:32.
[2] Mark 8:38.
[3] 1 Samuel 20:26–34.

and glorious majesty of the Man that is become our Advocate. Says the text, it is Jesus Christ—"We have an Advocate with the Father, Jesus Christ." Now, that he should become an Advocate, that he should embrace such an employ as this of his advocateship, let this be a wonderment, and so be accounted. But let us come to the fourth use.

Use Fourth. Is it so? Is Jesus Christ the Saviour also become our Advocate? Then let us labour to make that improvement of this doctrine as tendeth to strengthen our graces, and us, in the management of them. Indeed, this should be the use that we should make of all the offices of Christ; but let us, at this time, concern ourselves about this; let, I say, the poor Christian thus expostulate with himself—

1. Is Christ Jesus the Lord mine Advocate with the Father? Then awake, my faith, and shake thyself like a giant; stir up thyself, and be not faint; Christ is the Advocate of his people, and pleadeth the cause of the poor and needy. And as for sin, which is one great stumble to thy actings, O my faith, Christ has not only died for that as a sacrifice, nor only carried his sacrifice unto the Father, into the holiest of all, but is there to manage that offering as an Advocate, pleading the efficacy and worth thereof before God, against the devil, for us. Thus, I say, we should strengthen our faith; for faith has to do not only with the Word, but also with the offices of Christ. Besides, considering how many the assaults are that are made upon our faith, we find all little enough to support it against all the wiles of the devil.

Christians too little concern themselves, as I have said, with the offices of Jesus Christ; and therefore their knowledge of him is so little, and their faith in him so weak. We are bid to have our conversation in heaven, and then a man so hath, when he is there, in his spirit, by faith, observing how the Lord Jesus doth exercise his offices there for him. Let us often, by faith, go to the bar of God, there to hear our Advocate plead our cause; we should often have our faith to God's judgment seat, because we are concerned there; there we are accused of the devil, there we have our crimes laid open, and there we have our Advocate to plead; and this is suggested in the text, for it saith, "We have an Advocate with the Father;" therefore, thither our faith should go for help and relief in the day of our straits. I say, we should have our faith to God's judgment seat, and show it there, by the glass of our text,[1] what Satan is doing against, and the Lord Jesus for, our souls. We should also show it how the Lord Jesus carries away every cause from the devil, and from before the judgment seat, to the comfort of the children, the joy of angels, and the shame of the enemy. This would strengthen and support our faith indeed, and would make us more able than, for the most part, we are to apply the grace of God to ourselves, and hereafter to give more strong repulses to Satan. It is easy with a man, when he knows that his advocate has overthrown his enemy at the King's Bench bar or Court of Common Pleas, less to fear him the next time he sees him, and more boldly to answer him when he reneweth his threats on him. Let faith, then, be strengthened, from its being exercised about the advocateship of Jesus Christ.

2. As we should make use of Christ's advocateship for the strengthening of our faith, so we should also make use thereof to the encouraging us to prayer. As our faith is, so is our prayer; to wit, cold, weak, and doubtful, if our faith be so. When faith cannot apprehend that we have access to the Father by Christ, or that we have an Advocate, when charged before God for our sins by the devil, then we flag and faint in our prayer; but when we begin to take courage to believe—and then we do so when most clearly we apprehend Christ—then we get up in prayer. And according as a man apprehends Christ in his undertakings and offices, so he will wrestle with and supplicate God. As, suppose a man believes that Christ died for his sins; why, then, he will plead that in prayer with God. Suppose, also, that a man understands that Christ rose again for his justification; why, then, he will also plead that in prayer; but if he knows no more, no further will he go. But when he shall know that there is also for him an Advocate with the Father, and that that Advocate is Jesus Christ; and when the glory of this office of Christ shall shine in the face of this man's soul; oh, then, he takes courage to pray with that courage he had not before; yea, then is his faith so supported and made strong, that his prayer is more fervent, and importuning abundance. So that, I say, the knowledge of the advocateship of Christ is very useful to strengthen our graces; and, as of graces in general, so of faith and prayer in particular. Wherefore, our wisdom is,

---

[1] The Bible is the only perspective glass by which we can know futurity, and see things that, to carnal eyes, are invisible.—(Offor.)

so to improve this doctrine that prayer may be strengthened thereby.

3. As we should make use of this doctrine to strengthen faith and prayer, so we should make use of it to keep us humble; for the more offices Christ executeth for us with the Father, the greater sign that we are bad; and the more we see our badness, the more humble should we be. Christ gave for us the price of blood; but that is not all; Christ as a Captain has conquered death and the grave for us, but that is not all: Christ as a Priest intercedes for us in heaven; but that is not all. Sin is still in us, and with us, and mixes itself with whatever we do, whether what we do be religious or civil; for not only our prayers and our sermons, our hearings and preaching, and so; but our houses, our shops, our trades, and our beds, are all polluted with sin. Nor doth the devil, our night and day adversary, forbear to tell our bad deeds to our Father, urging that we might for ever be disinherited for this. But what should we now do, if we had not an Advocate; yea, if we had not one who would plead *in forma pauperis*; yea, if we had not one that could prevail, and that would faithfully execute that office for us? Why, we must die. But since we are rescued by him, let us, as to ourselves, lay our hand upon our mouth, and be silent, and say, "Not unto us, O Lord, not unto us, but unto thy name give glory." And, I say again, since the Lord Jesus is fain to run through so many offices for us before he can bring us to glory, oh! how low, how little, how vile and base in our own eyes should we be.

It is a shame for a Christian to think highly of himself, since Christ is fain to do so much for him, and he again not at all able to make him amends; but some, whose riches consist in nothing but scabs and lice, will yet have lofty looks. But are not they much to blame who sit lifting up of lofty eyes in the house, and yet know not how to turn their hand to do anything so, but that another, their betters, must come and mend their work? I say, is it not more meet that those that are such, should look and speak, and act as such that declare their sense of their unhandiness, and their shame, and the like, for their unprofitableness? yea, is it not meet that to every one they should confess what sorry ones they are? I am sure it should be thus with Christians, and God is angry when it is otherwise. Nor doth it become these helpless ones to lift up themselves on high. Let Christ's advocateship therefore teach us to be humble.

4. As we should improve this doctrine to strengthen faith, to encourage prayer, and keep us humble, so we should make use of it to encourage perseverance—that is, to hold on, to hold out to the end; for, for all those causes the apostle setteth Christ before us as an Advocate. There is nothing more discourages the truly godly than the sense of their own infirmities, as has been hinted all along; consequently, nothing can more encourage them to go on than to think that Christ is an Advocate for them. The services, also, that Christ has for us to do in this world are full of difficulty, and so apt to discourage: but when a Christian shall come to understand that—if we do what we can—it is not a failing either in matter or manner that shall render it wholly unserviceable, or give the devil that advantage as to plead thereby to prevail for our condemnation and rejection; but that Christ, by being our Advocate, saves us from falling short, as also from the rage of hell. This will encourage us to hold on, though we do but hobble in all our goings, and fumble in all our doings; for we have Christ for an Advocate in case we sin in the management of any duty—"If any man sin, we have an Advocate with the Father, Jesus Christ the righteous." Let us, therefore, go on in all God's ways as well as we can for our hearts; and when our foot slips, let us tell God of it, and his mercy in Christ shall hold us up.[1]

Darkness, and to be shut up in prison, is also a great discouragement to us; but our Advocate is for giving us light, and for fetching us out of our prison. True, he that Joseph chose to be his Advocate with Pharaoh remembered not Joseph, but forgat him,[2] but he that has Jesus Christ to be his Advocate shall be remembered before God,[3]—"He remembered us in our low estate; for his mercy *endureth* for ever."[4] Yea, he will say to the prisoners, Show yourselves; and to them that are in the prison-house, Go forth. Satan sometimes gets the saints into the prison when he has taken them captive by their lusts.[5] But they shall not be always there; and this should encourage us to go on in godly ways; for "we must through much tribulation enter into the kingdom of God."

Objection. But I cannot pray, says one, therefore how should

---

1 Psalm 84:9–12.
2 Genesis 40:14, 23.
3 Micah 7:8–10.
4 Psalm 136:23.
5 Romans 7:23.

I persevere? When I go to prayer, instead of praying, my mouth is stopped. What would you have me do?

Answer. Well, soul, though Satan may baffle thee, he cannot so serve thine Advocate; if thou must not speak for thyself, Christ thine Advocate can speak for thee. Lemuel was to open his mouth for the dumb—to wit, for the sons of destruction, and to plead the cause of the poor and needy.[1] If we knew the grace of our Lord Jesus Christ, so as the Word reveals it, we would believe, we would hope, and would, notwithstanding all discouragements, wait for the salvation of the Lord. But there are many things that hinder, wherefore faith, prayer, and perseverance, are made difficult things unto us—"But if any man sin, we have an Advocate with the Father, Jesus Christ the righteous;" and, God "shall fight for you, and you shall hold your peace," was once a good word to me when I could not pray.

5. As we should improve this doctrine for the improvement and encouragement of these graces, so we should improve it to the driving of difficulties down before us, to the getting of ground upon the enemy—"Resist the devil," drive him back; this is it for which thy Lord Jesus is an Advocate with God in heaven; and this is it for the sake of which thou art made a believer on earth.[2] Wherefore has God put this sword, WE HAVE AN ADVOCATE, into thy hand, but to fight thy way through the world? "Fight the good fight of faith, lay hold on eternal life," and say, "I will go in the strength of the Lord God." And since I have an Advocate with the Father, Jesus Christ the righteous, I will not despair, though "the iniquity of my heels shall compass me about."[3]

Use Fifth. Doth Jesus Christ stand up to plead for us with God, to plead with him for us against the devil? Let this teach us to stand up to plead for him before men, to plead for him against the enemies of his person and gospel. This is but reasonable; for if Christ stands up to plead for us, why should not we stand up to plead for him? He also expects this at our hands, saying, "Who will rise up for me against the evil doers? Who will stand up for me against the workers of iniquity?"[4] The apostle did it, and counted himself engaged to do it, where he

---

1 Proverbs 31:8–9.
2 1 Peter 5:9; Hebrews 12:4.
3 Psalm 49:5.
4 Psalm 94:16.

saith, he preached "the gospel of God with much contention."[1] Nor is this the duty of apostles or preachers only, but every child of God should "earnestly contend for the faith which was once delivered unto the saints."[2]

And, as I said, there is reason why we should do this; he standeth for us. And if we,

(1.) Consider the disparity of persons to plead, it will seem far more reasonable. He stands up to plead with God, we stand up to plead with men. The dread of God is great, yea, greater than the dread of men.

(2.) If we consider the persons pleaded for. He pleads for sinners, for the inconsiderable, vile, and base; we plead for Jesus, for the great, holy, and honourable. It is an honour for the poor to stand up for the great and mighty; but what honour is it for the great to plead for the base? Reason, therefore, requireth that we stand up to plead for him, though there can be but little rendered why he should stand up to plead for us.

(3.) He standeth up to plead for us in the most holy place, though we are vile; and why should we not stand up for him in this vile world, since he is holy?

(4.) He pleads for us, though our cause is bad; why should not we plead for him, since his cause is good?

(5.) He pleads for us, against fallen angels; why should we not plead for him against sinful vanities?

(6.) He pleads for us to save our souls; why should not we plead for him to sanctify his name?

(7.) He pleads for us before the holy angels; why should not we plead for him before princes?

(8.) He is not ashamed of us, though now in heaven; why should we be ashamed of him before this adulterous and sinful generation?

(9.) He is unwearied in his pleading for us; why should we faint and be dismayed while we plead for him?

My brethren, is it not reasonable that we should stand up for him in this world? yea, is it not reason that in all things we should study his exaltation here, since he in all things contrives our honour and glory in heaven? A child of God should study in every of his relations to serve the Lord Christ in this world, because Christ, by the execution of every one of his offices, seeks

---

1 1 Thessalonians 2:2.
2 Jude 3.

our promotion hereafter. If these be not sufficient arguments to bow us to yield up our members, ourselves, our whole selves to God, that we may be servants of righteousness unto him; yea, if by these and such like we are not made willing to stand up for him before men, it is a sign that there is but little, if any, of the grace of God in our hearts.

Yea, further, that we should have now at last in reserve Christ as authorized to be our Advocate to plead for us; for this is the last of his offices for us while we are here, and is to be put in practice for us when there are more than ordinary occasions. This is to help, as we say, at a dead lift, even then when a Christian is taken for a captive, or when he sinks in the mire where is no standing, or when he is clothed with filthy garments, or when the devil doth desperately plead against us our evil deeds, or when by our lives we have made our salvation questionable, and have forfeited our evidences for heaven. And why then should not we have also in *reserve* for Christ? And when profession and confession will not do, when loss of goods and a prison will not do, when loss of country and of friends will not do, then to bring it in, then to bring it in as the reserve, and as that which will do—to wit, willingly to lay down our lives for his name; and since he doth his part without grudging for us, let us do ours with rejoicing for him.[1]

Use Sixth. Doth Jesus Christ stand up to plead for us, and that of his mere grace and love? Then this should teach Christians to be watchful and wary how they sin against God. This inference seems to run retrograde; but whoso duly considers it, will find it fairly fetched from the premises. Christianity teaches ingenuity,[2] and aptness to be sensible of kindnesses, and doth instruct us to a loathness to be overhard upon him from whom we have all at free cost. "Shall we . . . sin that grace may abound? God forbid. Shall we do evil that good may come? God forbid. Shall we sin because we are not under the law, but under grace? God forbid."[3]

It is the most disingenuous thing in the world not to care how chargeable we are to that friend that bestows all upon us gratis. When Mephibosheth had an opportunity to be yet more chargeable to David, he would not, because he had his life and

---
1 Isaiah 24:15; John 21:19.
2 Ingenuity—ingenuousness, frankly, candidly, generously: now obsolete in this sense.—(Offor.)
3 Romans 6:1–2, 15.

his all from the mere grace of the king.¹ Also David thought it too much for all his household to go to Absalom's feast, because it was made of free cost. Why, Christ is our Advocate of free cost, we pay him neither fee nor income for what he doth; nor doth he desire aught of us, but to accept of his free doing for us thankfully; wherefore let us put him upon this work as little as may be, and by so doing we shall show ourselves Christians of the right make and stamp. We count him but a fellow of a very gross spirit that will therefore be lavishing of what is his friend's, because it is prepared of mere kindness for him; Esau himself was loath to do this; and shall Christians be disingenuous?

I dare say, if Christians were sober, watchful, and of a more self-denying temper, they need not put the Lord Jesus to that to which for the want of these things they do so often put him. I know he is not unwilling to serve us, but I know also that the love of Christ should constrain us to live not to ourselves, but to him that loved us, that died for us, and rose again.² We shall do that which is naught too much, even then when we watch and take care what we can to prevent it. Our flesh, when we do our utmost diligence to resist, it will defile both us and our best performances. We need not lay the reins on its neck and say, What care we? the more sin the more grace, and the more we shall see the kindness of Christ, and what virtue there is in his Advocate's office to save us. And should there be any such here, I would present them with a scripture or two; the first is this, "Do ye thus requite the Lord, O foolish people and unwise?"³ And if this gentle check will not do, then read the other, Shall we say, Let us do evil, that good may come? their damnation is just.⁴ Besides, as nothing so swayeth with us as love, so there is nothing so well pleasing to God as it. Let a man love, though he has opportunity to do nothing, it is accepted of the God of heaven. But where there is no love, let a man do what he will, it is not at all regarded.⁵ Now to be careless and negligent, and that from a supposed understanding of the grace of Christ in the exercise of his advocateship for us in heaven, is as clear sign as can be, that in thy heart there is no love to Christ,

---

1 2 Samuel 19:24–28.
2 2 Corinthians 5:14–15.
3 Deuteronomy 32:6.
4 Romans 3:8.
5 1 Corinthians 13:1–3.

and that consequently thou art just a nothing, instead of being a Christian. Talk, then, what thou wilt, and profess never so largely, Christ is no Advocate of *thine*, nor shalt thou, thou so continuing, be ever the better for any of those pleas that Christ, at God's bar, puts in against the devil, for his people.

Christians, Christ Jesus is not unwilling to lay out himself for you in heaven, nor to be an Advocate for you in the presence of his Father; but yet he is unwilling that you should render him evil for good; I say, that you should do so by your remissness and carelessness for want of such a thinking of things as may affect your hearts therewith. It would be more comely in you, would please him better, would better agree with your profession, and also better would prove you gracious, to be found in the power and nature of these conclusions. "How shall we that are dead to sin, live any longer therein?"[1] "If ye be risen with Christ, seek those things which are above, where Christ sitteth on the right hand of God; for ye are dead, and your life is hid with Christ in God. Mortify therefore your members which are upon the earth, fornication, uncleanness, inordinate affection, evil concupiscence, and covetousness, which is idolatry; for which things' sake the wrath of God cometh on the children of disobedience."[2]

I say, it would be more comely for Christians to say, We will not sin because God will pardon; we will not commit iniquity because Christ will advocate for us. "I write unto you that ye sin not; though if any man sin, we have an Advocate with the Father." Why, the brute would conclude, I will not do so, because my master will beat me; I will do thus, for then my master will love me. And Christians should be above [such] men, brutish men.

And for a conclusion as to this, let me present you with three considerations—

(1.) Know that it is the nature of grace to draw holy arguments to move to goodness of life from the love and goodness of God, but not thence to be remiss.[3]

(2.) Know therefore that they have no grace that find not these effects of the discoveries of the love and goodness of God.

(3.) Know also that among all the swarms of professors that from age to age make mention of the name of Christ, they only

---
1 Romans 6:2.
2 Colossians 3:1–6.
3 2 Corinthians 5:14.

must dwell with him in heaven that do part from iniquity, and are zealous of good works.[1] He gave himself for these.[2] Not that they were so antecedent to this gift. But those that he hath redeemed to himself are thus sanctified by the faith of him.[3]

Use Seventh. Is it so? Is Jesus Christ an Advocate with the Father for us? Then this should encourage strong Christians to tell the weak ones where, when they are in their temptations and fears through sin, they may have one to plead their cause. Thus the apostle doth by the text; and thus we should do one to another. Mark, he telleth the weak of an Advocate: "My little children, I write unto you," etc.

Christians, when they would comfort their dejected brethren, talk too much at rovers[4] or in generals; they should be more at the mark: "A word spoken in season, how good is it?" I say, Christians should observe and inquire, that they may observe the cause or ground of their brother's trouble; and having first taken notice of that, in the next place consider under which of the offices of Jesus Christ this sin or trouble has cast this man; and so labour to apply Christ in the word of the gospel to him. Sometimes we are bid to consider him as an Apostle and High Priest, and sometimes as a forerunner and an Advocate. And he has, as was said afore, these divers offices, with others, that we by the consideration of him might be relieved under our manifold temptations. This, as I said, as I perceive John teaches us here, as he doth a little before of his being a sacrifice for us; for he presenteth them that after conversion shall sin with Christ as an Advocate with the Father. As who should say, My brethren, are you tempted, are you accused, have you sinned, has Satan prevailed against you? "We have an Advocate with the Father, Jesus Christ the righteous."

Thus we should do, and deliver our brother from death. There is nothing that Satan more desires than to get good men in his sieve to sift them as wheat, that if possible he may leave them nothing but bran; no grace, but the very husk and shell of religion. And when a Christian comes to know this, should Christ as Advocate be hid, what could bear him up? But let him now remember and believe that "we have an Advocate with the

---

1 2 Timothy 2:19.

2 Titus 2:11–14.

3 Acts 26:18.

4 Rovers—without any definite aim. "Nature shoots not at *rovers*."—*Glanville.*
—(OFFOR.)

Father, Jesus Christ the righteous," and he forthwith conceiveth comfort; for an advocate is to plead for me according as has been showed afore, that I may be delivered from the wrath and accusation of my adversary, and still be kept safe under grace.

Further, by telling of my brother that he hath an Advocate, I put things into his mind that he has not known, or do bring them into remembrance which he has forgotten—to wit, that though he hath sinned, he shall be saved in a way of justice; for an advocate is to plead justice and law, and Christ is to plead these for a saint that has sinned; yea, so to plead them that he may be saved. This being so, he is made to perceive that by law he must have his sins forgiven him; that by justice he must be justified. For Christ as an Advocate pleadeth for justice, justice to himself; and this saint is of himself—a member of his body, of his flesh, and of his bones.

Nor has Satan so good a right to plead justice against us, though we have sinned, that we might be damned, as Christ has to plead it, though we have sinned, that we might be saved; for sin cannot cry so loud to justice as can the blood of Christ; and he pleads his blood as Advocate, by which he has answered the law; wherefore the law having nothing to object, must needs acquit the man for whom the Lord Jesus pleads. I conclude this with that of the Psalmist, "Surely his salvation *is* nigh them that fear him; that glory may dwell in our land. Mercy and truth are met together; righteousness and peace have kissed *each other*. Truth shall spring out of the earth; and righteousness shall look down from heaven. Yea, the Lord shall give *that which is* good; and our land shall yield her increase. Righteousness shall go before him; and shall set *us* in the way of his steps."[1]

Use Eighth. But what is all this to you that are not concerned in this privilege? The children, indeed, have the advantage of an advocate; but what is this to them that have none to plead their cause?[2] they are, as we say, left to the wide world, or to be ground to powder between the justice of God and the sins which they have committed. This is the man that none but the devil seeks after; that is pursued by the law, and sin, and death, and has none to plead his cause. It is sad to consider the plight that such an one is in. His accuser is appointed, yea, ordered to bring in a charge against him—"Let Satan stand at

---

1 Psalm 85:9–13.
2 Jeremiah 30:12–13.

his right hand," in the place where accusers stand. "And when he shall be judged, let him be condemned," let there be none to plead for his deliverance. If he cries, or offereth to cry out for mercy or forgiveness, "let his prayer become sin."[1] This is the portion of a wicked man: "terrors take hold on him as waters, a tempest stealeth him away in the night, the east wind carrieth him away, and he departeth, and as a storm hurleth him out of his place; for *God* shall cast upon him, and not spare; he would fain flee out of his hand. *Men* shall clap their hands at him, and shall hiss him out of his place."[2] And what shall this man do? Can he overstand the charge, the accusation, the sentence, and condemnation? No, he has none to plead his cause. I remember that somewhere I have read, as I think, concerning one who, when he was being carried upon men's shoulders to the grave, cried out as he lay upon the bier, I am accused before the just judgment of God; and a while after, I am condemned before the just judgment of God. Nor was this man but strict as to the religion that was then on foot in the world; but all the religion of the world amounts to no more than nothing, I mean as to eternal salvation, if men be denied an Advocate to plead their cause with God. Nor can any advocate save Jesus Christ the righteous avail anything at all, because there is none appointed but him to that work, and therefore not to be admitted to enter a plea for their client at the bar of God.

Objection. But some may say, There is God's grace, the promise, Christ's blood, and his second part of priesthood now in heaven. Can none of these severally, nor all of them jointly, save a man from hell, unless Christ also become our Advocate?

Answer. All these, his Advocate's office not excluded, are few enough, and little enough, to save the saints from hell; for the righteous shall scarcely be saved.[3] There must, then, be the promise, God's grace, Christ's blood, and him to advocate too, or we cannot be saved. What is the promise without God's grace, and what is that grace without a promise to bestow it on us? I say, what benefit have we thereby? Besides, if the promise and God's grace, without Christ's blood, would have saved us, wherefore then did Christ die? Yea, and again I say, if all these, without his being an Advocate, would have delivered us from

---

1 Psalm 109:6–7.
2 Job 27:20–23.
3 1 Peter 4:18.

all those disadvantages that our sins and infirmities would bring us to and into; surely in vain and to no purpose was Jesus made an Advocate. But, soul, there is need of all; and therefore be not thou offended that the Lord Jesus is of the Father made so much to his, but rather admire and wonder that the Father and the Son should be so concerned with so sorry a lump of dust and ashes as thou art. And I say again, be confounded to think that sin should be a thing so horrible, of power to pollute, to captivate, and detain us from God, that without all this ado (I would speak with reverence of God and his wisdom) we cannot be delivered from the everlasting destruction that it hath brought upon the children of men.

But, I say, what is this to them that are not admitted to a privilege in the advocate-office of Christ? Whether he is an Advocate or no, the case to them is the same. True, Christ as a Saviour is not divided; he that hath him not in all, shall have him in none at all of his offices in a saving manner. Therefore, he for whom he is not an Advocate, he is nothing as to eternal life.

Indeed, Christ by some of his offices is concerned for the elect, before by some others of them he is; but such shall have the blessing of them all before they come to glory. Nor hath a man ground to say Christ is here or there mine, before he hath ground to say, he also is mine Advocate; though that office of his, as has been already showed, stands in the last place, and comes in as a reserve. But can any imagine that Christ will pray for them as Priest for whom he will not plead as Advocate? or that he will speak for them to God for whom he will not plead against the devil? No, no; they are his own, that he loveth to the end,[1] to the end of their lives, to the end of their sins, to the end of their temptations, to the end of their fears, and of the exercise of the rage and malice of Satan against them. To the end may also be understood, even until he hath given them the profit and benefit of all his offices in their due exercise and administration. But, I say, what is all this to them that have him not for their Advocate?

You may remember that I have already told you that there are several who have not the Lord Jesus for their Advocate—to wit, those that are still in their sins, pursuing of their lusts; those that are ashamed of him before men; and those that are never otherwise but lukewarm in their profession. And let us

---

1 John 13:1.

now, for a conclusion, make further inquiry into this matter.

Is it likely that those should have the Lord Jesus for their Advocate to plead their cause; who despise and reject his person, his Word, and ways? or those either who are so far off from sense of, and shame for, sin, that it is the only thing they hug and embrace? True, he pleadeth the cause of his people both with the Father and against the devil, and all the world besides; but open profaneness, shame of good, and without heart or warmth in religion, are no characters of his people. It is irrational to think that Christ is an Advocate for, or that he pleadeth the cause of such, who, in the self-same hour, and before his enemies, are throwing dirt in his face by their profane mouths and unsanctified lives and conversations.

If he pleads as an Advocate for any, he must plead against Satan for them, and so consequently must have some special bottom to ground his plea upon; I say, a bottom better than that upon which the carnal man stands; which bottom is either some special relation that this man stands in to God, or some special law he hath privilege by, that he may have some ground for an appeal, if need be, to the justice and righteousness of God; but none of these things belong to them that are dead in trespasses and sins; they stand in no special relation to God: they are not privileged by the law of grace.

Objection.—But doth not Christ as Advocate plead for his elect, though not called as yet?

Answer.—He died for all his elect, he prayeth for all his elect as a Priest, but as an Advocate he pleadeth only for the children, the *called* only. Satan objecteth not against God's election, for he knows it not; but he objecteth against the called—to wit, whether they be truly godly or no, or whether they ought not to die for their transgressions.[1] And for these things he has some colour to frame an accusation against us, and now it is time enough for Christ to stand up to plead. I say, for these things he has some colour to frame a plea against us; for there is sin and a law of works, and a judge too, that has not respect of persons. Now to overthrow this plea of Satan, is Jesus Christ our Advocate; yea, to overthrow it by pleading law and justice; and this must be done with respect to the children only—"My little children, these things write I unto you, that ye sin not. And if any man sin, we have an Advocate with the Father, Jesus Christ the righteous."

---

[1] Job 1:9–10; Zechariah 3.

www.ingramcontent.com/pod-product-compliance
Lightning Source LLC
Chambersburg PA
CBHW031448040426
42444CB00007B/1021